COOKING FOR
SPECIAL OCCASIONS

GOOD HOUSEKEEPING
STEP-BY-STEP COOKERY

COOKING FOR SPECIAL OCCASIONS

Guild Publishing/Ebury Press
LONDON

First published 1984 by
Book Club Associates
By arrangement with Ebury Press

This edition published 1986

Consultant editor: Jeni Wright
Editor: Miren Lopategui
Design by Roger Daniels
Drawings by John Woodcock
Photographs by Paul Kemp

The Publishers would especially like to thank Jane Kemp and Divertimenti
for their help in providing accessories for photography.

Cover photograph: Beef Wellington (page 34), Green Beans with Coconut (page 99),
Hasselback Potatoes (page 157) and Individual Chocolate Mousses (page 113)

Filmset by Advanced Filmsetters (Glasgow) Ltd

Printed and bound in Italy by
New Interlitho, S.p.a., Milan

CONTENTS

COOKERY NOTES

Follow either metric or imperial measures for the recipes in this book as they are not inter-changeable. Sets of spoon measures are available in both metric and imperial size to give accurate measurement of small quantities. All spoon measures are level unless otherwise stated. When measuring milk we have used the exact conversion of 568 ml (1 pint).

* Size 4 eggs should be used except when otherwise stated.

† Granulated sugar is used unless otherwise stated.

● All recipes in this book serve six people unless otherwise stated.

OVEN TEMPERATURE CHART

°C	°F	Gas mark
110	225	$\frac{1}{4}$
130	250	$\frac{1}{2}$
140	275	1
150	300	2
170	325	3
180	350	4
190	375	5
200	400	6
220	425	7
230	450	8
240	475	9

KEY TO SYMBOLS

1.00* Indicates minimum preparation and cooking times in hours and minutes. They do not include prepared items in the list of ingredients; calculated times apply only to the method. An asterisk * indicates extra time should be allowed, so check the note immediately below the symbols.

⬠ Chef's hats indicate degree of difficulty of a recipe: no hat means it is straightforward; one hat slightly more complicated; two hats indicates that it is for more advanced cooks.

£ Indicates a recipe which is good value for money; £ £ indicates an expensive recipe.

✳ Indicates that a recipe will freeze. If there is no symbol, the recipe is unsuitable for freezing. An asterisk * indicates special freezer instructions so check the note immediately below the symbols.

309 cals Indicates calories per serving, including any serving suggestions (e.g. pitta bread, to serve) given in the list of ingredients.

METRIC CONVERSION SCALE

	LIQUID				SOLID		
Imperial	Exact conversion	Recommended ml		Imperial	Exact conversion	Recommended g
$\frac{1}{4}$ pint	142 ml	150 ml		1 oz	28.35 g	25 g
$\frac{1}{2}$ pint	284 ml	300 ml		2 oz	56.7 g	50 g
1 pint	568 ml	600 ml		4 oz	113.4 g	100 g
$1\frac{1}{2}$ pints	851 ml	900 ml		8 oz	226.8 g	225 g
$1\frac{3}{4}$ pints	992 ml	1 litre		12 oz	340.2 g	350 g

For quantities of $1\frac{3}{4}$ pints and over, litres and fractions of a litre have been used.

Imperial	Exact conversion	Recommended g
14 oz	397.0 g	400 g
16 oz (1 lb)	453.6 g	450 g

1 kilogram (kg) equals 2.2 lb.

COOKING FOR
SPECIAL OCCASIONS

Planning a wedding reception? Throwing a cocktail party? Or just having a few friends round for a cosy dinner? Don't be daunted by the prospect or stuck for ideas. Simply turn the pages of this book and you'll find an absolute host of wonderful, inspiring ways to make special occasion food – from the wickedly extravagant and exotic to budget-conscious dishes that look and taste expensive. Clear step-by-step illustrations take you through the methods without a single hitch.

How to use this book
Dinner party dishes are here in profusion, with separate sections on pre-dinner snacks, starters, main courses, vegetables and desserts, each recipe with its own menu suggestion so you don't have to think of a thing.

Literally every special occasion is also covered: large and formal receptions with cold finger food, smaller, more informal buffet parties with hot main dishes, fun ideas for children's birthdays, summertime barbecue spreads, traditional afternoon tea parties and all the Christmas fare.

Turn to the back of the book and you'll find all the informative material you need to make entertaining at home a success: how to cope with large numbers, how to plan menus and prepare ahead, how to write invitations, set tables, present food prettily, and serve the drinks. Plus lots of basic recipes for food and drink which make this a complete guide to home entertaining.

Soups and Starters

Your choice of dinner party starter is a very important one: first impressions will linger throughout the meal. A starter that can be prepared in advance is a boon to the busy cook, leaving time on the night for last-minute cooking of the main course. Plan your starter along with the other courses which follow, and try to achieve a happy balance of flavour, colour and texture.

CHESTNUT AND ORANGE SOUP

| *1.00* | £ | ✳ | 199 cals |

450 g (1 lb) whole chestnuts

40 g (1½ oz) butter

125 g (4 oz) carrots, peeled and finely chopped

2 onions, skinned and finely chopped

125 g (4 oz) mushrooms, wiped and finely chopped

5 ml (1 tsp) plain flour

1.4 litres (2½ pints) beef stock

salt and freshly ground pepper

15 ml (1 tbsp) finely grated orange rind

3 Melt the butter in a large saucepan, add the vegetables and fry together until lightly browned. Add the flour and cook, stirring, for a further 3–4 minutes or until the flour begins to colour.

4 Off the heat, stir in the stock, prepared chestnuts and seasoning. Bring slowly to the boil, stirring. Simmer, covered, for 40–45 minutes or until the chestnuts are quite tender.

5 Cool a little, then purée in a blender or a food processor, a small quantity at a time. Add half the orange rind and reheat for serving. Adjust seasoning and garnish with the remaining orange rind.

Menu Suggestion
Serve with Boned Stuffed Poussins (page 66) and Fresh Pear Short-cake (page 118).

1 Nick the brown outer skins of the chestnuts with a pair of sharp kitchen scissors, or the tip of a sharp knife.

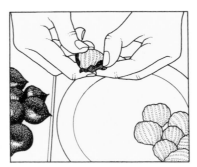

2 Cook the chestnuts in boiling water for 3–5 minutes, then lift out, a few at a time, using a slotted spoon. Peel off both the outer and inner skins and discard.

SWEET CHESTNUTS
These grow prolifically all over the Mediterranean, and are a common feature of many of the local cuisines – the Italians and the French have so many of them they even grind them into flour. Sweet chestnuts are grown in Britain, but most of the ones we see in the shops come from Spain and France – the French ones called *marrons* being the most highly prized.

AVOCADO WITH PARMA HAM

| 0.10 | £ £ | 401 cals |

50 g (2 oz) Parma ham
90 ml (6 tbsp) vegetable oil
45 ml (3 tbsp) lemon juice
5 ml (1 tsp) Dijon mustard
salt and freshly ground pepper
3 spring onions, finely chopped
3 ripe avocados
hot French bread, to serve

1 With lightly oiled kitchen scissors, cut the ham into fine shreds. Whisk the oil, lemon juice, mustard and seasoning together.

2 Stir in the spring onions and the ham. Cut the avocados in half and twist to remove the stones; put each half on a plate. If necessary, cut a thin slice off the base of each one so that it stands level on the serving plate.

3 Spoon the ham mixture into the avocados. Serve at once with hot French bread, if wished.

Menu Suggestion
Serve with Baked Trout with Lemon (page 77) and Almond and Coffee Meringue Cake (page 107).

FETA CHEESE SOUFFLÉ

| 1.00 | £ | 207 cals |

butter, for greasing
grated Parmesan cheese
25 g (1 oz) butter
30 ml (2 tbsp) plain flour
200 ml (7 fl oz) milk
salt and freshly ground pepper
225 g (8 oz) Feta cheese, grated
50 g (2 oz) stuffed olives, chopped
4 eggs, separated

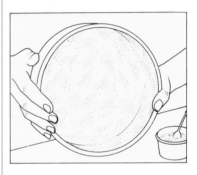

1 Lightly butter a 1.7-litre (3-pint) soufflé dish and dust out with the grated Parmesan.

2 Melt the butter in a saucepan, add the flour and cook for 1 minute, stirring. Off the heat, gradually stir in the milk and black pepper. Bring to the boil; cook for 2–3 minutes, stirring. Allow to cool slightly, then beat in the Feta, olives and egg yolks. Season.

3 Whisk the egg whites until stiff and beat a large spoonful into the sauce. Lightly fold in the rest and pour the mixture into the dish.

4 Bake in the oven at 180°C (350°F) mark 4 for about 40 minutes or until the soufflé is golden. Serve immediately.

Menu Suggestion
Serve with Guard of Honour (page 40) and Almond Peach Brulée (page 116).

MOUSSELINE OF SOLE WITH PRAWNS

1.10* 🍴🍴 £ £ 572 cals

* plus 3 hours chilling

450 g (1 lb) fillets of sole, skinned
  and chopped

50 g (2 oz) shelled prawns

1 egg white, beaten

1.25 ml ($\frac{1}{4}$ tsp) salt

1.25 ml ($\frac{1}{4}$ tsp) ground white
  pepper

450 ml (15 fl oz) double cream

3 egg yolks

75 g (3 oz) unsalted butter,
  softened

10 ml (2 tsp) lemon juice

5 ml (1 tsp) tomato purée

whole prawns, to garnish

1 Combine the chopped fish with
  the prawns, egg white and
seasoning. Purée the mixture in a
blender or food processor with
300 ml (10 fl oz) cream.

2 Oil six 150-ml ($\frac{1}{4}$-pint) oven-
  proof ramekins and press the
mixture well down into the dishes.
Cover each dish with a round of
foil pleated in the centre; chill for
3 hours.

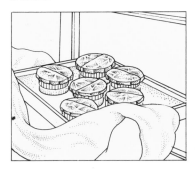

3 Place the ramekins in a large
  roasting tin and half fill with
boiling water. Bake in the oven at
150°C (300°F) mark 2 for 30–40
minutes. Stand on a wire rack to
drain. Keep warm.

4 Over a pan of hot water, combine yolks, a knob of butter
and lemon juice. Whisk until thick.
Remove from heat; add remaining
butter and tomato purée. Add remaining cream, whipped, return
to heat, without boiling. Turn out,
add sauce and garnish.

Menu Suggestion
Serve with Beef in Brandy and
Mustard (page 36) and Melon and
Ginger Sorbet (page 47).

CAULIFLOWER AND ALMOND CREAM SOUP

1.00*	✳	306 cals

* plus 2 hours soaking

few saffron strands
60 ml (4 tbsp) boiling water
100 g (4 oz) flaked almonds
50 g (2 oz) butter
1 onion, skinned and chopped
450 g (1 lb) cauliflower florets
1.3 litres (2¼ pints) chicken stock
freshly grated nutmeg
salt and freshly ground pepper
150 ml (5 fl oz) double cream

1 Soak the saffron in the boiling water for 2 hours. Toast half the almonds on a sheet of foil under the grill, turning them frequently. Leave to cool.

2 Melt the butter in a large saucepan, add the onion and fry gently until soft. Add the cauliflower and the untoasted almonds and stir, cover and cook gently for 10 minutes.

3 Add the stock and stir well, then strain in the yellow saffron liquid. Add a pinch of nutmeg and salt and pepper to taste. Bring to the boil, then lower the heat, cover and simmer for 30 minutes or until the cauliflower is very tender.

4 Purée the soup in a blender until very smooth (you may have to do this twice to break down the almonds). Return to the rinsed-out pan, add half the cream and reheat gently. Taste and adjust seasoning, then pour into a tureen.

5 Swirl in the remaining cream and sprinkle with the toasted almonds and a little nutmeg, if liked. Serve immediately.

Menu Suggestion
Serve the soup with Guard of Honour (page 40) and Raspberry Pavlova (page 90).

STUFFED GLOBE ARTICHOKES

1.30	🝙	£ £	518 cals

6 medium globe artichokes

45 ml (3 tbsp) lemon juice

salt and freshly ground pepper

2 onions, skinned and finely chopped

350 g (12 oz) rindless streaky bacon, finely sliced

75 g (3 oz) butter

700 g (1½ lb) ripe tomatoes, skinned

175 g (6 oz) fresh white breadcrumbs

finely grated rind and juice of 2 medium oranges

90 ml (6 tbsp) chopped fresh parsley

2 eggs

melted butter, to serve

1 Strip away discoloured leaves. Slice off stem of artichoke as close as possible to the base of leaves. Level up so artichokes stand upright.

2 Using scissors, snip off the leaf tips. Soak the artichokes in cold water acidulated with 15 ml (1 tbsp) lemon juice for about 30 minutes while preparing the rest.

3 Drain artichokes and place them in a large pan of boiling salted water with the remaining lemon juice.

4 Cover and boil gently for 30–45 minutes, depending on size. The artichokes will float, so turn them during cooking and keep covered, to steam the leaves above the water.

5 Meanwhile, make the stuffing. Fry the onions and bacon in the butter until onions are soft and bacon golden. Quarter, seed and roughly chop tomatoes.

6 Add the tomatoes to the pan, cook for a few minutes, then stir in the crumbs, grated orange rind, parsley, eggs and seasoning, beating well to mix.

7 Test whether the artichokes are cooked. To do this, gently pull an outer leaf; if cooked, it will come out easily.

8 Drain the cooked artichokes upside down in a colander and hold briefly under cold tap. This helps to bring out and set the green colour and cools down the leaves for handling.

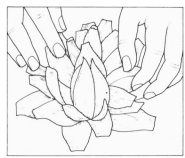

9 Gradually peel back leaves, working from the outside inwards (be careful not to snap any off). Continue peeling back the leaves until the hairy choke of the artichoke is exposed.

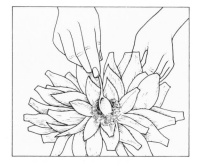

10 With a teaspoon, scrape away and discard hairs. Hollow out heart slightly.

11 Spoon stuffing generously over hearts; divide it evenly between the six artichokes.

12 Gently fold the leaves back around the stuffing. Tie string around each one to hold it together.

13 Pack artichokes into a well-buttered deep ovenproof dish or shallow casserole. Pour over strained orange juice and cover tightly with buttered grease-proof paper or foil and the lid. Bake in the oven at 190°C (375°F) mark 5 for 25 minutes. To serve, remove string and offer melted butter separately.

Menu Suggestion
Serve with Lamb with Almonds (page 38) and Mango Ice Cream (page 112).

ITALIAN SQUID SALAD

| 2.00* 🍴🍴 £ £ | 394 cals |

* including 1 hour standing time

1.25–1.5-kg (2½–3-lb) squid

6 garlic cloves, skinned and crushed with 5 ml (1 tsp) salt

300 ml (½ pint) full-bodied Italian red wine

300 ml (½ pint) water

½ onion, skinned and finely sliced

1 red pepper, cored, seeded and thinly sliced

1 green pepper, cored, seeded and thinly sliced

135 ml (9 tbsp) olive oil

juice of 1 lemon

700 g (1½ lb) prawns in their shells or 225 g (8 oz) peeled prawns and 12 whole prawns to garnish

one 50-g (2-oz) can anchovies in oil, drained and soaked in milk 20 minutes

15 ml (1 tbsp) chopped fresh basil, or 10 ml (2 tsp) dried

freshly ground pepper

few large lettuce leaves

fresh basil sprigs and black olives, to garnish

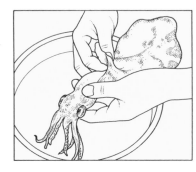

1 Clean the squid. Hold under cold running water to rinse thoroughly. Pull back the edge of the body pouch to expose the translucent quill or pen.

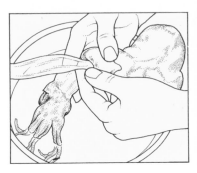

2 Holding the body pouch firmly with one hand, take hold of the end of the exposed quill with the other and pull it free. Then discard the quill.

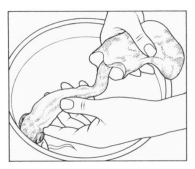

3 Separate the tentacles from the body pouch. Holding the body pouch in one hand, pull out the head and tentacles with the other.

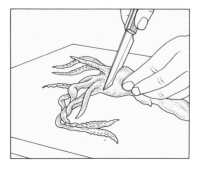

4 Cut through the head, just above the eyes. Discard the eyes and ink sac and reserve the tentacles until required.

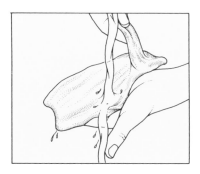

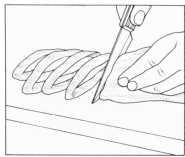

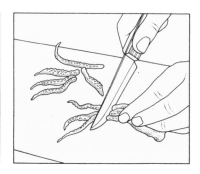

5 Rub the purplish skin off the body pouch and tentacles, holding them under cold running water. Discard the skin.

6 Using a sharp knife, carefully cut the triangular fins off the body pouch. Discard the fins and cut the body into thin rings.

7 Cut the reserved tentacles into small pieces. If they are very small, leave some whole.

8 Put all the squid pieces in an earthenware baking dish. Add half the garlic. Pour over the wine and water, then cover and cook in the oven at 180°C (350°F) mark 4 for 1½–2 hours until tender. Cool.

9 Drain the squid, then rinse quickly under cold running water and drain again thoroughly. Put into a bowl with the remaining garlic, the onion, red and green peppers, olive oil and lemon juice. Stir well to mix.

10 Peel the prawns, if using whole prawns, reserving twelve whole ones for the garnish. Drain the anchovies, rinse and pat dry on absorbent kitchen paper, then chop them roughly.

11 Add the peeled prawns to the salad with the anchovies, basil and pepper to taste. Fold gently to mix, then cover and leave to stand for about 1 hour.

12 To serve, line a bowl with lettuce leaves and pile the squid into the centre. Garnish with the reserved whole prawns, and basil sprigs and black olives.

Menu Suggestion
Serve with Pork Loin with Cider (page 43) and Raspberry and Apple Torte (page 115).

DUCK PÂTÉ EN CROÛTE BIGARADE

| 3.45* 🔲 🔲 £ £ ✳ | 485 cals |

* plus 1 hour standing time plus overnight chilling

Serves 12

| 450 g (1 lb) pork belly |
| 3-kg (6-lb) duckling |
| 225 g (8 oz) chicken livers |
| 100 g (4 oz) white breadcrumbs |
| grated rind and juice of orange |
| 60 ml (4 tbsp) brandy |
| 2 garlic cloves |
| 6 black peppercorns |
| 6 juniper berries |
| 6 coriander seeds |
| 5 ml (1 tsp) salt |
| 275 g (10 oz) streaky bacon, rinded |
| 225 g (8 oz) middle-cut bacon rashers, rinds removed |
| 453-g (16-oz) can cherries, drained |
| 225 g (8 oz) packet frozen puff pastry or 100 g (4 oz) home-made (see page 152) |
| 1 egg, beaten |

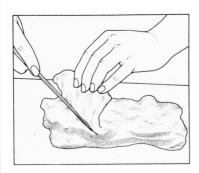

1 Remove skin from pork and cut meat and fat into small pieces. Bone the duckling (see page 158) and cut all the meat into small pieces except the breast.

2 Mince duck and pork pieces in a food processor with livers. Turn into a bowl, add bread-crumbs, orange rind and juice and half the brandy and stir well. Pound garlic and spices to a paste. Add to duck mixture with salt and mix. Cover; set aside for 1 hour.

3 Meanwhile, place the duck breasts in a shallow dish and pour over the remaining brandy. Cover; set aside for 1 hour.

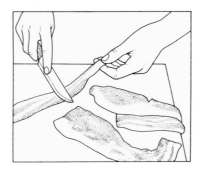

4 With the flat of a large knife, stretch the streaky bacon rashers and the streaky end of the middle-cut bacon. Use about three-quarters to line the base and sides of a 20-cm (8-inch) round cake tin.

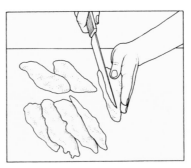

5 Put half the duck mixture in the tin. Drain the suprêmes and cut horizontally into thin slices. Cover the duck mixture with half the duck slices and half of remaining middle-cut bacon.

6 Arrange the cherries in a single layer over the top, then cover with the remaining duck slices and middle-cut bacon.

7 Put the remaining duck mix-ture on top, pressing it down firmly, then top with the remaining stretched bacon.

8 Cover the tin with foil, then place in a roasting dish half filled with hot water. Bake in the oven at 180°C (350°F) mark 4 for 2½ hours or until the juices run clear when the pâté is tested with a skewer.

9 Carefully drain off the fat and cooking juices, then cover with a plate and place heavy weights on top. Cool overnight.

10 The next day, roll out the pastry on a lightly floured surface into a circle large enough to enclose the pâté completely. Reserve pastry trimmings.

11 Turn the pâté out of the tin and scrape off any jelly or sediment. Brush the pastry lightly with beaten egg, then place the pâté in the centre.

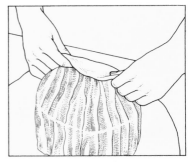

12 Wrap in the pastry, then place join side down on a dampened baking sheet. Brush with beaten egg, then decorate with pastry trimmings and brush these with egg.

13 Bake in the oven at 200°C (400°F) mark 6 for 25 minutes until golden. Leave to cool before serving.

Menu Suggestion
Serve the duck pâté with Chicken with Tarragon Mayonnaise (page 60) and Individual Chocolate Mousses (page 113).

SMOKED SALMON AND TROUT MOUSSES

0.45	🥣 🥣	£ £	484 cals

450 g (1 lb) pink trout, cleaned

300 ml (½ pint) milk

bay leaf and 6 peppercorns for
flavouring

15 ml (3 tsp) gelatine

45 ml (3 tbsp) water

25 g (1 oz) butter

30 ml (2 tbsp) plain flour

salt and freshly ground pepper

15 ml (1 tbsp) Dijon mustard

20 ml (4 tsp) tomato ketchup

175–225 g (6–8 oz) thinly sliced
smoked salmon

150 ml (¼ pint) mayonnaise

30 ml (2 tbsp) lemon juice

150 ml (5 fl oz) double cream

black olives and lemon slices, to
garnish

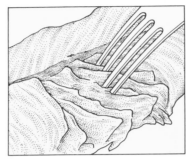

1 Poach the trout in the milk
with flavourings for about 20
minutes until tender. Drain;
reserve the milk. Discard head,
skin and bone and flake the fish.

2 Soak the gelatine in the water.
Make a white sauce (page 154)
from the fat, flour and reserved
milk. Season and stir in soaked
gelatine until dissolved.

3 In a blender or food processor,
blend the sauce, fish, mustard
and ketchup to form a smooth
purée; cool.

4 Line six lightly oiled 175 ml
(6 fl oz) ramekin dishes with
the smoked salmon. Whip the
cream until softly stiff. Stir the
mayonnaise, lemon juice and
cream into the fish mixture.
Adjust seasoning.

5 Spoon into the dishes, cover
and refrigerate to set. Turn out
the mousses and garnish with
lemon slices and black olives.

Menu Suggestion
Serve with Beef Wellington (page
34) and Individual Chocolate
Mousses (page 113).

CREAM OF LEMON SOUP

| 1.00 | £ | ✳ | 109 cals |

25 g (1 oz) butter

2 onions, skinned and thinly sliced

75 g (3 oz) carrot, peeled and thinly sliced

75 g (3 oz) celery, trimmed and thinly sliced

2 lemons

1.1 litres (2 pints) chicken stock

2 bay leaves

salt and freshly ground pepper

150 ml (5 fl oz) single cream

spring onion tops or chives and lemon slices, to garnish

pitta bread, to serve

1 Melt the butter in a large saucepan and add the vegetables. Cover the pan and stew gently for 10–15 minutes until vegetables begin to soften.

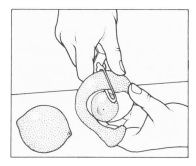

2 Meanwhile, thinly pare the lemons using a potato peeler. Blanch the rinds in boiling water for 1 minute, drain. Squeeze the juice from the lemons to give 75–90 ml (5–6 tbsp).

3 Add the rind and juice, stock and bay leaves; season. Bring to the boil, cover and simmer for 40 minutes or until the carrots and celery are both very soft.

4 Cool the soup a little, remove the bay leaves, then purée the pan contents in a blender or food processor until quite smooth.

5 Return the soup to the clean pan, reheat gently, stirring in the cream. Do not boil. Adjust seasoning to taste. Serve hot or chilled, garnished with chopped spring onions or chives and lemon slices, and serve with pitta bread.

Menu Suggestion
Serve with Moussaka (page 46) and Mango Ice Cream (page 112).

CHILLED ASPARAGUS SOUP

| 1.00* | £ £ | ✳ | 310 cals |

* plus refrigeration time

700 g (1½ lb) stalks of asparagus

salt and freshly ground pepper

50 g (2 oz) butter or margarine

225 g (8 oz) onions, skinned and thinly sliced

1.4 litres (2½ pints) chicken stock

30 ml (2 tbsp) chopped fresh parsley

150 ml (5 fl oz) single cream

small brown uncut loaf, fresh butter, for spreading

lemon slices, to garnish

1 Rinse the asparagus. Cut off the heads and simmer very gently in salted water until just tender. Drain carefully and cool; cover and refrigerate until required to make asparagus rolls.

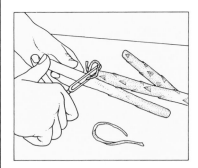

2 Scrape the asparagus stalks with a potato peeler or knife to remove any scales; cut off the woody ends. Thinly slice the asparagus stalks.

3 Melt the butter or margarine in a large saucepan. Add the asparagus and onions, cover and cook over a moderate heat for 5–10 minutes or until the vegetables are beginning to soften.

4 Add the stock and parsley, season and bring to the boil. Cover and simmer for 30 minutes, or until the asparagus and onion are quite tender. Cool slightly.

5 Purée in a blender or food processor until smooth. Sieve if necessary. Cool, then stir in the cream and adjust seasoning. Cover and chill well before serving.

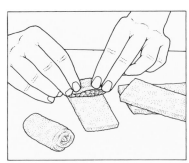

6 Cut six thin slices of brown bread and butter them. Cut off the crusts and halve lengthwise. Roll asparagus heads inside each piece of bread; place on a serving plate, cover with cling film and refrigerate until required.

7 Serve the soup well chilled, garnished with wafer thin lemon slices and accompanied by the asparagus rolls.

Menu Suggestion
Serve with Rump Steak in Whisky (page 37) and Raspberry Pavlova (page 90).

ASPARAGUS
This vegetable is sold graded according to the thickness of its stems, usually in bundles, but sometimes by the kg/lb. The thicker the stems the more expensive the asparagus; for making soups it is not essential to buy the best grades. For use in cooked dishes or soups, look for the small, thin green asparagus called 'sprue', which is the least expensive grade.

MEXICAN AVOCADO DIP

| 0.15 | £ £ | 383 cals |

30 ml (2 tbsp) vegetable oil

1 small onion, skinned and finely
  chopped

2 garlic cloves, skinned and
  crushed

2.5 ml ($\frac{1}{2}$ tsp) chilli powder

4 tomatoes, skinned and chopped

2 ripe avocados

juice of $\frac{1}{2}$ lemon

142 ml (5 fl oz) soured cream

salt and freshly ground black
  pepper

tomato slices, to garnish

1 Heat oil in a small pan, add
  the onion, garlic and chilli and
fry gently, stirring, until onion is
soft. Add the tomatoes and fry for
a further 5 minutes, breaking them
up with a wooden spoon.

2 Put the tomato mixture into a
  blender or food processor and
blend until smooth. Turn into a
bowl and leave to cool.

3 Halve and stone the avocados,
  then peel three halves. Add to
the tomato mixture with the lemon
juice and mash to a purée. Blend
in half the soured cream, then
taste and add salt and pepper and
more chilli powder, if liked.

4 Transfer the dip to a shallow
  serving bowl. Peel and slice
the remaining avocado half.
Arrange avocado slices on top of
dip, alternating with tomato slices.

5 To serve, spoon the remaining
  cream into the centre and
sprinkle with a little chilli powder.
Serve immediately.

Menu Suggestion
Serve with Veal in Marsala (page
47) and Fresh Pear Shortcake
(page 118).

SNACKS AND FINGER FOODS

SPICED MINI MEATBALLS WITH PEANUT DIP

| 0.35 | £ | ✳* | 80 cals |

* meatballs will freeze; dip will not

75 g (3 oz) block creamed coconut, broken into pieces

120 ml (8 tbsp) boiling water

60 ml (4 tbsp) crunchy peanut butter

30 ml (2 tbsp) soft brown sugar

5 ml (1 tsp) chilli sauce

salt and freshly ground pepper

450 g (1 lb) fine or ground minced beef

30 ml (2 tbsp) natural yogurt

30 ml (2 tbsp) soy sauce

5 ml (1 tsp) ground coriander

5 ml (1 tsp) ground turmeric

5 ml (1 tsp) olive or vegetable oil

vegetable oil, for deep frying

1 Make the dip. Put the coconut in a saucepan, add the boiling water and stir until the coconut has dissolved. Add the next three ingredients and season to taste; stir over gentle heat until thick and well combined. Remove from the heat and set aside.

2 Make the meatballs. Put the remaining ingredients in a bowl and season to taste. Mix with your hands until well combined, squeezing the mixture so that it clings together.

3 Form the mixture into about fifty bite-sized balls by rolling heaped teaspoonfuls in the palms of your hands.

4 Heat the oil in a deep-fat frier to 190°C (375°F). Add the meatballs about 10 at a time and deep-fry for 1–2 minutes only until lightly coloured. Remove with a slotted spoon and drain on absorbent kitchen paper while frying the remainder.

5 Spear each meatball with a cocktail stick. Reheat the dip, stirring constantly to keep smooth. Pour the dip into a small bowl and place in the centre of a large, circular platter. Arrange the meatballs around the bowl of dip. Serve both meatballs and dip hot.

ANCHOVY CRESCENTS

| 0.45 | f ✳* | 337 cals |

* freeze before frying

175 g (6 oz) full fat soft cheese

two 50-g (2-oz) cans anchovies, drained and soaked in milk for 20 minutes

finely grated rind of 2 lemons

30 ml (2 tbsp) finely chopped fresh parsley

1.25–2.5 ml ($\frac{1}{4}$–$\frac{1}{2}$ tsp) paprika, according to taste

freshly ground pepper

368-g (13-oz) packet frozen puff pastry, thawed or 225 g (8 oz) homemade (see page 152)

vegetable oil, for deep-frying

grated Parmesan cheese, to finish (optional)

1 Put the cheese in a bowl and beat until creamy. Drain the anchovies, rinse and pat dry with absorbent kitchen paper. Mash them roughly, then add them to the cheese with the lemon rind and parsley. Add paprika and pepper to taste and beat well to mix.

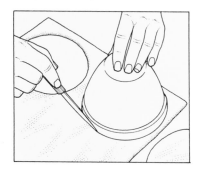

2 Roll out half the pastry on a lightly floured surface and cut out seven to eight 12-cm (5-inch) circles using a basin or small plate as a guide. Halve each circle.

3 Brush the edges of one semi-circle with water, then fold in half and seal the straight edge to make a cone shape.

4 Fill each cone with about 5 ml (1 tsp) of the cheese mixture, then press and crimp the top edge to seal. Repeat with the remaining semi-circles, then roll out and repeat with the remaining half of the dough, to make about thirty crescents in all.

5 Heat the oil in a deep-fat frier to 190°C (375°F). Lower the crescents into the oil a few at a time and deep-fry for 1–2 minutes until puffed up and golden brown.

6 Remove with a slotted spoon and drain on absorbent paper while frying the remainder. Sprinkle with Parmesan and paprika while still hot, if liked. Serve warm.

MUSHROOM SAVOURIES

| 0.15* | f | 33 cals |

* plus 2–3 hours chilling

450 g (1 lb) button mushrooms, wiped

25 g (1 oz) butter

50 g (2 oz) fresh brown breadcrumbs

20 ml (4 tsp) mango chutney

salt and pepper

seasoned flour

2 eggs, size 2, beaten

grated Parmesan cheese

mayonnaise, to serve

1 Chop the mushroom stalks finely. Melt the butter in a pan, stir in the stalks and half the crumbs. Sauté for 2–3 minutes. Off the heat, stir in the chutney; season.

2 Sandwich two mushroom caps together with a little of the mixture. Roll the mushrooms in seasoned flour, dip in egg and coat with the remaining breadcrumbs mixed with 50 g (2 oz) grated Parmesan. Chill for 2–3 hours.

3 Deep-fry for 3–4 minutes until golden brown. Drain well and roll in Parmesan. Leave to cool completely. Serve on cocktail sticks with mayonnaise.

Afternoon Tea Party for 20 People

SACHERTORTE

(*Make 2*)

PARTY PINWHEELS

CHEESY PÂTÉ CHEQUERBOARDS

SALMON AND PARMA ROLLUPS

GLAZED FRUIT BOATS

SACHERTORTE

1.10	£ £	456 cals

Serves 10

200 g (7 oz) plain chocolate

175 g (6 oz) unsalted butter

100 g (4 oz) caster sugar

100 g (4 oz) ground almonds

4 eggs, separated

50 g (2 oz) fresh brown
  breadcrumbs

30 ml (2 tbsp) apricot jam, melted
  and sieved

50 g (2 oz) icing sugar

10 ml (2 tsp) hot water

chocolate curls, to decorate

1 Line the base of a 23-cm (9-inch) spring release cake tin
and brush with melted butter.
Break half the chocolate into a
bowl. Place the bowl over a pan
of simmering water and stir until
melted. Remove from the heat.

2 Cream 125 g (4 oz) butter and
the sugar together until light
and fluffy. Add the almonds. Stir
in the egg yolks, breadcrumbs and
the melted chocolate. Beat the ingredients well together.

3 Whisk the egg whites until stiff
and fold half into the chocolate
mixture, then fold in the remaining egg whites. Pour into the prepared tin and level the surface.

4 Bake the cake in the oven at
180°C (350°F) mark 4 for
40–45 minutes until it is firm to
the touch.

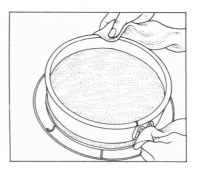

5 Cover with a damp tea-towel,
leave for 5 minutes to cool
slightly then unclip the sides
and invert on to a wire rack. Remove the base. Turn the cake
uppermost and cover again. Leave
the cake until cold. Brush the top
with the melted apricot jam.

6 Melt the remaining chocolate
with the remaining butter in a
bowl over simmering water. Remove the bowl from the heat. Sift
in the icing sugar and mix well.
Stir in the water and leave to stand
for 5 minutes.

7 Spread the icing on top of the
cake, easing it gently to the
edge to cover the sides. Leave to
set then sprinkle with chocolate
curls to decorate.

GLAZED FRUIT BOATS

0.45*	🍴 🍴	164 cals

* plus 1 hour chilling

Makes 24

250 g (9 oz) plain flour

pinch of salt

125 g (4½ oz) unsalted butter

15 g (½ oz) caster sugar

egg, beaten

3 egg yolks

75 g (3 oz) caster sugar

25 ml (1½ tbsp) plain flour

25 ml (1½ tbsp) cornflour

450 ml (¾ pint) milk

25 ml (1½ tbsp) Strega liqueur

about 100 g (4 oz) green grapes, halved and seeded

about 100 g (4 oz) black grapes, halved and seeded

30 ml (2 tbsp) sieved lime marmalade

30 ml (2 tbsp) water

30 ml (2 tbsp) redcurrant jelly

1 Make the pastry. Sift the flour and salt into a bowl. Add the butter in small pieces, then rub in until the mixture resembles fine breadcrumbs. Stir in the sugar, then the beaten egg. Mix to a smooth dough. Wrap and refrigerate for about 30 minutes.

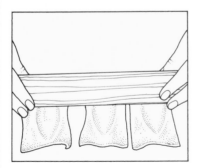

2 Roll out the dough on a lightly floured surface and use to line 24 large barquette moulds. Prick bases with a fork, then stand on baking sheets and chill again in the refrigerator for 30 minutes.

3 Bake in the oven at 180°C (350°F) mark 4 for 15–20 minutes until pastry is crisp and lightly coloured. Leave until cold.

4 Make the *crème patissière*. Mix the egg yolks, sugar and flours together with a little milk. Scald remaining milk, pour in a thin, steady stream on to egg yolk mixture, then return to pan and simmer until thick and smooth.

5 Cover with cling film and leave until cold. Stir in the liqueur, then spoon a little into each boat. Top half the boats with green grapes and the other half with black, making sure the *crème patissière* is covered.

6 Heat the marmalade with 15 ml (1 tbsp) water, stirring, then brush over green grapes. Repeat with redcurrant jelly and remaining water and brush over black grapes. Leave to cool and set, then refrigerate until serving time. Serve chilled.

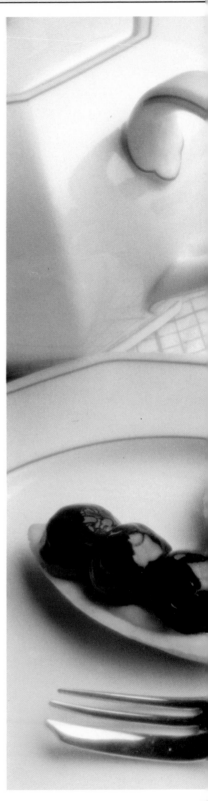

PARTY PINWHEELS

| 0.15* | £ | ✳ | 84 cals |

* plus 1 hour chilling

Makes about 100

350 g (12 oz) full fat soft cheese at
    room temperature

200-g (7-oz) can shrimps, drained

juice of ½ lemon

1.25 ml (¼ tsp) cayenne pepper

about 5 ml (1 tsp) tomato purée

salt and freshly ground pepper

1 bunch watercress, finely chopped

finely grated rind of 1 orange

30 ml (2 tbsp) fresh orange juice

large fresh white sandwich loaf

softened butter, for spreading

large wholemeal sandwich loaf

1 Divide the cheese in half and
put into separate bowls. Mash
the shrimps, then beat into one
bowl of cheese with lemon juice
and cayenne. Add enough tomato
purée to colour pink. Season.

2 Beat the watercress into the
other bowl of cheese. Add the
orange rind and juice, to make
a spreading consistency. Add salt
and pepper to taste.

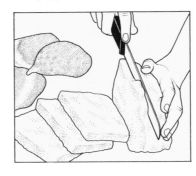

3 Cut the crusts off the white
loaf, then cut into seven slices
lengthways. Spread each slice liberally with butter, right to the
edges, then spread each with the
shrimp filling.

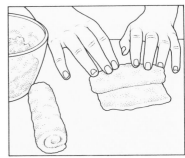

4 Roll up each slice from one
short end, then wrap each one
individually in cling film. Refrigerate for 1 hour. Repeat step 3 with
the wholemeal loaf, butter and
watercress filling. Roll up, wrap
and refrigerate as with the shrimp
filling.

5 Unwrap the rolls and cut each
one across into about eight
slices. Arrange on a sandwich
plate, alternating colours.

CHEESY PÂTÉ CHEQUERBOARDS

| 0.15* | £ | 49 cals |

* plus 1 hour chilling

Makes 60

15 slices white bread

10 large slices dark rye bread

4 eggs, hard-boiled, finely mashed

175 g (6 oz) Red Leicester cheese,
    finely grated

about 60 ml (4 tbsp) mayonnaise

English mustard powder, to taste

salt and freshly ground pepper

softened butter, for spreading

175 g (6 oz) fine liver pâté

1 Cut the crusts off the bread.
Place a slice of rye bread on
top of a slice of white bread and
trim them to the same size. Repeat
with remaining slices. Mix eggs
and cheese, add enough mayonnaise for a spreading consistency.
Add mustard, salt and pepper.

2 Spread one slice of white bread
with butter right to the edges.
Spread generously with filling, top
with a slice of rye. Butter the rye
right to the edges, then spread
with pâté. Repeat layers once more.

3 Spread one slice of white
bread with butter, then place
buttered side down on top of pâté
filling. Wrap closely in cling film
and refrigerate for at least 1 hour.

4 Make four more layered sandwiches in this way, wrapping
them in cling film and putting
them in the refrigerator as you
make them.

5 Just before serving, unwrap
each sandwich and cut into four
lengthways. Cut each piece across
into three, to make twelve chequerboards from each sandwich. Arrange on a plate and serve.

SALMON AND PARMA ROLLUPS

0.15	£ £	34 cals

Makes about 40

100 g (4 oz) unsalted butter
45 ml (3 tbsp) chopped fresh herbs
10 ml (2 tsp) French mustard
freshly ground black pepper
10 slices smoked salmon
20 slices Parma ham
two 425-g (15-oz) cans asparagus,
   drained and trimmed
lemon wedges, to garnish

1 Beat the butter to a spreading consistency with the herbs, mustard and pepper to taste. Cut the salmon slices in half lengthways. Spread a little of mixture over salmon.

2 Place an asparagus spear at one end. Roll the salmon up around the asparagus to enclose it completely, letting the tip of the asparagus protrude slightly at the end of the roll. Try to make them an even size.

3 Repeat with the remaining salmon and asparagus, then with the ham. Place rolls on a serving platter, arranging them in a circle radiating out from the centre. Garnish with lemon and refrigerate before serving.

Parma Ham

Parma ham or *prosciutto* is world famous and needs little introduction. The *prosciutto* from Parma is reputed to be the best. It should be pale red in colour, sweet and tender, and it should be thinly cut. In Italy *prosciutto* is eaten with melon, the scented deep yellow kind, or with fresh figs, green or black.

MAIN COURSES

Meat

The main course of a dinner party is often neglected by the busy cook, sandwiched as it is between the first course which needs to make a spectacular start to the meal, and the dessert which is the grand finale.

When planning your dinner party menu, think carefully about the main course dish, especially if it is to be meat, since accurate timing is all important.

BEEF WELLINGTON

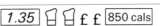 `1.35` 🍴 🍴 £ £ `850 cals`

1.4 kg (3 lb) fillet of beef
freshly ground pepper
100 g (4 oz) butter
225 g (8 oz) button mushrooms, sliced
175 g (6 oz) smooth liver pâté
368-g (13-oz) packet frozen puff pastry, thawed, or 225 g (8 oz) homemade (see page 152)
beaten egg, to seal and glaze

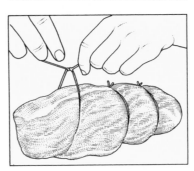

1 Trim and tie up the fillet of beef at regular intervals to retain its shape, and season with freshly ground pepper. Melt 50 g (2 oz) butter in a large frying pan. When the butter is foaming, add the meat and fry briskly on all sides to colour. Press down with a wooden spoon while frying, to seal the surface well.

2 Place the fried fillet of beef in the oven and roast at 220°C (425°F) mark 7 for 20 minutes. Leave beef to cool and remove the string.

3 Meanwhile, sauté the mushrooms in remaining butter until soft; leave until cold, then mix with the pâté.

4 Roll the pastry out to a large rectangle about 33 × 28 cm (13 × 11 inches) and 0.5 cm ($\frac{1}{4}$ inch) thick.

5 Spread the pâté mixture down the centre of the pastry. Place the meat in the centre. Brush the edges of the pastry with egg.

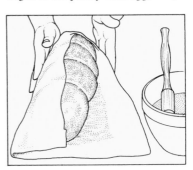

6 Fold the pastry edges over lengthways and turn the parcel over so that the join is underneath. Fold the ends under the meat on a baking sheet.

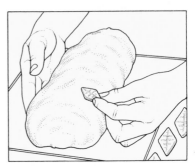

7 Decorate with leaves cut from the pastry trimmings. Chill until pastry is firm; just before baking, brush with egg. Cook at 220°C (425°F) mark 7 for 50 minutes, covering with foil after 25 minutes.

Menu Suggestion
Serve with Avocado with Parma Ham (page 10) and Gooseberry Charlotte (page 110).

BEEF IN BRANDY AND MUSTARD

| 2.00 | £ £ ✳* | 477 cals |

* freeze before step 4

1.1-kg (2½-lb) piece chuck steak
30 ml (2 tbsp) vegetable oil
50 g (2 oz) butter
2 onions, skinned and chopped
60 ml (4 tbsp) brandy
1 garlic clove, skinned and crushed
15 ml (1 tbsp) whole grain mustard
300 ml (½ pint) beef stock
salt and freshly ground pepper
225 g (8 oz) celery, trimmed
50 g (2 oz) walnut halves
75 ml (5 tbsp) single cream

1 Cut the piece of chuck steak into thin strips about 0.5 cm (¼ inch) wide and 3.5 cm (1½ inches) long.

2 Heat the oil with 25 g (1 oz) butter in a medium flameproof casserole and brown the meat well; take out and drain.

3 Add the onion to the reheated pan juices and fry until golden; return the meat to the casserole and flame with the brandy. Stir in garlic with mustard, stock and seasoning and bring to the boil.

4 Cover the dish tightly and cook in the oven at 150°C (300°F) mark 2 for about 1½ hours or until the meat is quite tender.

5 Cut the celery diagonally into fine strips and, just before serving time, sauté with the walnuts in the remaining butter until golden.

6 Add the walnut mixture to the meat and bring to the boil, stirring; simmer for 2–3 minutes and drizzle cream over the top before serving.

Menu Suggestion
Serve with Mousseline of Sole with Prawns (page 12) and Almond and Coffee Meringue Cake (page 107).

RUMP STEAK IN WHISKY

0.20* £ £ 309 cals
* plus 12 hours marinating

**1.1-kg (2½-lb) piece rump steak,
   about 2 cm (¾ inch) thick**

**1 small onion, skinned and thinly
   sliced**

2 garlic cloves, skinned

90 ml (6 tbsp) whisky

30 ml (2 tbsp) vegetable oil

freshly ground pepper

salt

watercress sprigs, to garnish

1 Trim off any excess fat from the steak, then place the meat in an edged dish into which it will just fit comfortably.

2 Scatter onion over meat. To make the marinade, crush the garlic and mix with the whisky, oil and pepper. Pour over meat. Cover tightly with cling film and refrigerate for at least 12 hours, turning and basting once.

3 Preheat the grill. Lift the meat out of the marinade and pat the surface dry with absorbent kitchen paper, then place on the rack of the grill pan.

4 Grill the rump steak under a high heat for about 6 minutes each side, depending on how rare you like it.

5 Meanwhile, strain the marinade into a small saucepan and warm gently; adjust seasoning, adding salt at this stage if necessary.

6 Lift the steak on to a serving plate and spoon over the warmed liquid. To serve, garnish the steak with watercress sprigs.

Menu Suggestion
Serve with Salmon and Parma Rollups (page 33) and Fresh Pear Shortcake (page 118).

LAMB WITH ALMONDS

| 1.45 | £ £ | 597 cals |

2-kg (4½-lb) leg of lamb on the bone

60 ml (4 tbsp) vegetable oil

2 onions, skinned and finely chopped

15 ml (1 tbsp) ground ginger

5 ml (1 tsp) paprika

75 g (3 oz) ground almonds

75 ml (3 fl oz) chicken stock

300 ml (10 fl oz) single cream

1 garlic clove, skinned and crushed

salt and freshly ground pepper

25 g (1 oz) fresh root ginger

chopped fresh parsley, to garnish

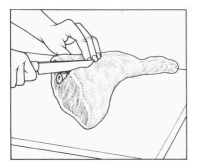

1 Using a sharp knife, carefully remove the meat from the bone of the leg of lamb, scraping the meat until the entire bone of the leg is exposed.

2 Cut the meat into 2.5-cm (1-inch) pieces, making sure to thoroughly discard the skin and any excess fat.

3 Heat the oil in a medium flameproof casserole and brown the meat a little at a time. Remove meat from the casserole using draining spoons and set aside.

4 Add the onion to the residual oil and sprinkle over the ground ginger and paprika. Cook gently for 1 minute, stirring.

5 Mix in the almonds, stock, cream, garlic and seasoning and bring to the boil. Replace the meat, stir well, cover tightly and cook in oven at 170°C (325°F) mark 3 for 1¼ hours.

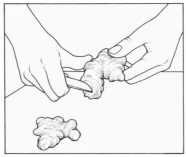

6 Peel root ginger and chop finely; stir into the lamb dish, re-cover and return to the oven for a further 20 minutes, or until the meat is quite tender. Skim well, adjust seasoning and serve garnished with chopped parsley.

Menu Suggestion
Serve with Iced Tzaziki Soup (page 86) and Mango Ice Cream (page 112).

--- VARIATION ---

This recipe requires about 1.1 kg (2½ lb) lean boned meat. If you want to use shoulder of lamb instead of leg, buy 2.5 kg (5½ lb) to allow for wastage when boning and trimming off fat.

For a Middle Eastern flavour, use **ground allspice** instead of ground ginger, omit the root ginger, and use **50 g (2 oz) pine nuts** instead of the almonds. Add these nuts 20 minutes before the end of cooking time.

GUARD OF HONOUR

2.15 | 🍳 🍳 £ £ | 564 cals

2 best end necks of lamb, chined,
    each with 6–7 cutlets
eating apple, peeled and cored
25 g (1 oz) butter or margarine
small onion, skinned and chopped
stick of celery, trimmed and
    chopped
25 g (1 oz) dried apricots, soaked
50 g (2 oz) white breadcrumbs
30 ml (2 tbsp) chopped fresh
    parsley
finely grated rind of $\frac{1}{2}$ lemon and
    15 ml (1 tbsp) fresh lemon juice
egg yolk
salt and freshly ground pepper
50 g (2 oz) lard
30 ml (2 tbsp) plain flour
450 ml ($\frac{3}{4}$ pint) beef stock

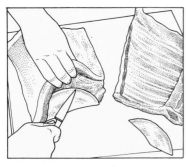

1 Cut away the chine bones and
ease out the shoulder blades
from both joints.

2 Trim away the flesh between
each cutlet bone and scrape the
bone ends clean to a depth of
2.5 cm (1 inch).

3 Stand the lamb joints up, with
the fat side outside, then inter-
lace the cutlet bones to form an
arch.

4 To make the stuffing, chop the
apple and sauté in butter until
browning, together with the onion
and celery. Drain, dry and chop
the apricots and stir into the pan
with the next five ingredients.
Season well, cool.

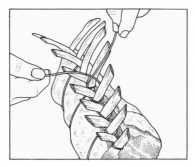

5 Fill the cavity of the lamb with
the stuffing. Tie the bones
together in two or three places and
cover the exposed bones with foil.
Season with salt and pepper.
Weigh the joint.

6 Stand the joint in a roasting tin
with the lard. Roast in the
oven at 180°C (350°F) mark 4 for
30 minutes to the 450 g (1 lb), plus
30 minutes. Baste occasionally and
cover lightly with foil, if necessary.

7 Place the rack of lamb on a
warm serving dish, remove foil
from bone ends and keep warm in
a low oven. Pour off all but 30 ml
(2 tbsp) fat from the roasting tin.
Stir in the flour and cook for about
5 minutes until just brown.
Gradually stir in the stock. Bring
to the boil, then simmer for 2–3
minutes. Adjust seasoning and
serve separately.

Menu Suggestion
Serve with Chilled Asparagus
Soup (page 22) and Boodle's
Orange Fool (page 55).

PORK LOIN WITH CIDER

| 2.40 | 🍴 🍴 £ £ | 926 cals |

600 ml (1 pint) dry cider

1.8 kg (4 lb) loin of pork, boned,
  with rind on

salt

2 onions, skinned

125 g (4 oz) rindless streaky bacon

50 g (2 oz) butter

225 g (8 oz) button or cup
  mushrooms, wiped and chopped

5 ml (1 tsp) dried rubbed sage

125 g (4 oz) fresh white
  breadcrumbs

1 egg, beaten

freshly ground pepper

30 ml (2 tbsp) vegetable oil

175 g (6 oz) carrots, peeled and
  cut into matchsticks

2 bay leaves

15 ml (1 tbsp) cornflour

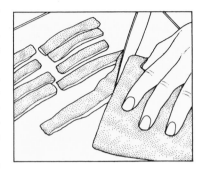

1 Pour the cider into a small pan and boil to reduce by half. Remove the rind and most of the fat from the pork and cut into thin fingers. Place these in a small roasting tin. Add salt; set aside.

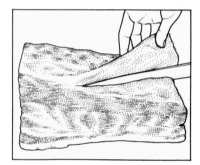

2 Slit the loin of pork along the eye of the meat three-quarters of the way through, from the centre outwards. Open out so that it forms a long roll.

3 To make the stuffing, chop one of the onions and snip the bacon into small pieces.

4 Melt half the butter in a medium frying pan, add the bacon and onion and cook slowly until the bacon fat runs and the ingredients begin to brown. Increase the heat, add the mushrooms and cook until all excess moisture has evaporated.

5 Turn out into a large bowl and stir in the sage, breadcrumbs and enough egg to bind. Season, mix well and cool.

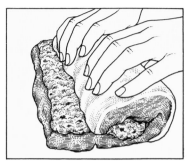

6 Spread the cold stuffing over the pork, roll up and tie at regular intervals. Slice the remaining onion. Heat the oil in a flameproof casserole, add the remaining butter and brown the joint. Remove from pan.

7 Add the sliced onion and carrots to the residual fat and lightly brown. Replace the meat and pour the reduced cider around. Stir in the bay leaves and seasoning and bring to the boil.

8 Cover tightly and place on a low shelf in the oven at 170°C (325°F) mark 3. Place the roasting tin of pork rind and fat above and cook both for about 2 hours.

9 Lift the pork out of the casserole with any stuffing that has oozed out and slice, discarding string. Remove vegetables from casserole and arrange on the serving plate with the sliced pork, cover and keep warm.

10 Mix the cornflour to a smooth paste with a little water and stir into the pan juices. Bring to the boil, stirring. Cook for 2 minutes. To serve, garnish with the crackling strips. Serve the gravy separately.

Menu Suggestion
Serve the pork loin with Avocado and Kiwi Fruit Vinaigrette (page 125) and Raspberry and Apple Torte (page 115).

43

ROAST PORK TENDERLOIN

| 2.00 | £ £ | 458 cals |

175 g (6 oz) button mushrooms, wiped and roughly chopped

1 onion, skinned and finely chopped

50 g (2 oz) butter

125 g (4 oz) fresh brown breadcrumbs

5 ml (1 tsp) dried rubbed sage

salt and freshly ground pepper

1 egg, size 3, beaten

3 pork tenderloins, about 900 g (2 lb) total weight

125 g (4 oz) thin rashers streaky bacon

150 ml ($\frac{1}{4}$ pint) dry white wine

300 ml ($\frac{1}{2}$ pint) chicken stock

10 ml (2 tsp) arrowroot

parsley sprigs, to garnish

1 To make the stuffing, fry the mushrooms and onion in 25 g (1 oz) hot butter until golden, take off the heat. Mix in the bread-crumbs and sage with plenty of seasoning and enough egg to bind, and leave to cool.

2 Carefully trim any skin and excess fat from the pork tenderloins and slit lengthwise, three-quarters of the way through each tenderloin. Open the meat out so that it is as flat as possible.

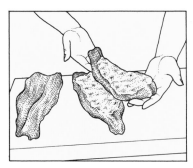

3 Spread one piece of meat with half of the mushroom mixture. Top with one of the tenderloins. Add remaining stuffing and top with remaining tenderloin.

4 Snip rind off bacon and stretch out each rasher thinly. Wrap up meat in bacon rashers and tie with string to form a "joint".

5 Put the pork parcel in a small roasting tin and spread remaining butter over the top; season well. Pour the wine around and roast at 180°C (350°F) mark 4 for about 1$\frac{3}{4}$ hours, basting frequently. Lift on to a platter, and remove string. Keep warm.

6 Add stock to pan and boil up well. Blend arrowroot with a little water to a smooth paste and add to pan, stirring all the time. Bubble for 1 minute, adjust seasoning. Garnish with parsley.

Menu Suggestion
Serve with Stuffed Globe Arti-chokes (page 14) and Almond and Peach Brulée (page 116).

MOUSSAKA

2.00	£	✳	495 cals

450 g (1 lb) aubergines, sliced

salt

90 ml (6 tbsp) vegetable oil

2 large onions, skinned and sliced

garlic clove, skinned and chopped

700 g (1½ lb) fresh minced beef or lamb

396-g (14-oz) can tomatoes

freshly ground pepper

284 g (10 oz) natural yogurt

2 eggs, size 3, beaten

1.25 ml (¼ tsp) grated nutmeg

25 g (1 oz) grated Parmesan cheese

1 Layer the aubergine slices in a colander, sprinkling each layer with salt. Then cover and leave for about 30 minutes.

2 Meanwhile, heat 30 ml (2 tbsp) oil in a frying pan and fry onions and garlic for 5 minutes. Add meat and fry for 10 minutes. Add tomatoes with their juice, season and simmer for 20 minutes.

3 Drain the aubergine slices, rinse and dry well. In a separate large frying pan, cook for 4–5 minutes in the remaining oil, turning once. Add more oil, if there is not enough for frying.

4 Arrange a layer of aubergine in the bottom of a large oven-proof dish and spoon over a layer of meat. Continue the layers until all the meat and aubergines are used, finishing with aubergines.

5 Beat the yogurt, eggs, seasoning and nutmeg together and stir in half the Parmesan. Pour over the dish and sprinkle with the remaining cheese.

6 Bake the moussaka in the oven at 180°C (350°F) mark 4 for about 45 minutes until golden.

Menu Suggestion
Serve with Iced Tzaziki Soup (page 86) and Almond Peach Brulée (page 116).

DÉGORGER
To sprinkle aubergine slices with salt is called *dégorger*. The salt brings out the bitter juices present in the flesh of aubergines which, if left in, would make the finished moussaka taste sour and unpalatable. For maximum effect, always *dégorge* aubergines for 30 minutes before cooking (no matter what the dish) and rinse and dry thoroughly afterwards.

VEAL IN MARSALA

| 0.25 | £ £ | 301 cals |

| 6 small veal escalopes, about 75 g (3 oz) each |
| salt and freshly ground pepper |
| flour, for coating |
| 60 ml (4 tbsp) vegetable oil |
| 50 g (2 oz) butter |
| 1 onion, skinned and finely chopped |
| 175 g (6 oz) button mushrooms, wiped and sliced |
| 90 ml (6 tbsp) Marsala |
| 90 ml (6 tbsp) chicken stock |
| 5 ml (1 tsp) arrowroot |
| lemon wedges, to garnish |

1 Trim each escalope to remove any skin. Place well apart between sheets of non-stick paper, or heavy duty cling film.

2 Bat out well, using a meat mallet, rolling pin or heavy-based pan, until the escalopes are very thin. Remove paper or film.

3 Toss the veal in the seasoned flour. Then heat the oil and butter in a large sauté or deep frying pan and brown the veal well on all sides.

4 Push to the side of the pan and brown the onion and mushrooms in the residual fat. Add the Marsala, stock and bring to the boil; season lightly.

5 Cover the pan and cook gently for 5–10 minutes or until the veal is quite tender. Transfer to a serving dish, cover and keep warm.

6 Mix the arrowroot to a smooth paste with a little water. Stir into the pan juices off the heat, then bring slowly to the boil, stirring all the time. Cook for 1 minute, adjust seasoning and spoon over the veal. Garnish with lemon wedges.

Menu Suggestion
Serve with Italian Squid Salad (pages 16–17) and Crêpes Annette (page 108).

Marsala
This famous Sicilian wine is made from a blend of local wines, brandy and unfermented grape juice. There are dry as well as sweet Marsalas, though the sweet variety used for classic Italian dishes, such as *zabaglione*, is most widely available.

Though it is a dessert wine, it is also an effective pick-me-up at any time of day.

FRICASSEE OF VEAL

| 1.45 | £ £ ✳* | 441 cals |

* freeze before step 8

900 g (2 lb) stewing veal

450 g (1 lb) carrots, peeled

1 onion, skinned

15 ml (1 tbsp) chopped fresh thyme
or 2.5 ml (½ tsp), dried

150 ml (¼ pint) dry white wine

900 ml (1½ pints) water

salt and freshly ground pepper

50 g (2 oz) butter

50 g (2 oz) plain flour

6 rashers streaky bacon

2 egg yolks

150 ml (5 fl oz) single cream

1 Cut the veal into 4-cm (1½-inch) squares. Cover the meat with cold water, bring to the boil and bubble for 1 minute.

2 Strain the veal through a colander and clean. Rinse out the pan thoroughly and replace the pieces of meat.

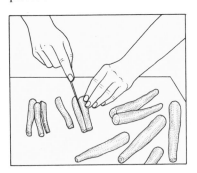

3 Cut the carrots into finger-sized pieces and slice the onion. Add to the pan with the thyme, wine, water and seasoning.

4 Bring slowly to the boil, cover and simmer gently for about 1¼ hours or until the veal is quite tender.

5 Strain off the cooking liquid, make up to 750 ml (1¼ pints), with water or stock if necessary, and reserve; keep the veal and vegetables warm in a covered serving dish.

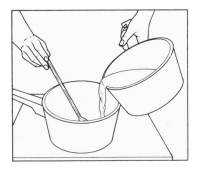

6 Melt the butter and stir in the flour, cook gently for 1 minute. Off the heat, stir in the strained cooking liquid, season well and bring to the boil, stirring all the time. Cook the sauce gently for 5 minutes.

7 Carefully remove the rinds from the streaky bacon and roll up the rashers. Then grill the bacon rolls.

8 Mix the egg yolks with the cream; take the sauce off the heat and stir in the cream mixture. Return to the heat and warm gently – without boiling – until the sauce becomes slightly thicker.

9 To serve, adjust seasoning. Pour the cream sauce over the meat and serve garnished with the bacon rolls.

Menu Suggestion
Serve with Italian Squid Salad (pages 16–17) and Individual Chocolate Mousses (page 113).

FRICASSEE
This recipe for Fricassee of Veal is very typically French – the word *fricassée* is used for any dish which is cooked in a white sauce or stock (often made with white wine). Usually white meats such as veal and chicken are cooked in *fricassées*, although other meats and fish and vegetables are also sometimes cooked this way. *Blanquette* is another French term which means virtually the same as *fricassée*.

LIAISON
The thickening of the sauce with egg yolks and cream just before serving is also typically French. Known as a *liaison*, it is used in *fricassées* and *blanquettes* rather than the other methods of thickening with *beurre manié* (a paste of butter and flour) or cornflour, to give a richer, creamier result.

Anniversary Buffet for 15 to 20 People

CRISPY CHICKEN NIBBLES

| 0.50* | £ | ✳* | 30 cals |

* plus 1 hour standing time and
  2 hours refrigeration; freeze
  before frying

Makes about 100

**6 boneless chicken breasts, total
  weight about 900 g (2 lb), skinned**

75 ml (5 tbsp) soy sauce

10 ml (2 tsp) ground ginger

5 ml (1 tsp) English mustard

90 ml (6 tbsp) plain flour

3 eggs, beaten

350 g (12 oz) white breadcrumbs

75 g (3 oz) sesame seeds

vegetable oil, for deep-frying

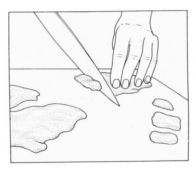

1 Cut the chicken into about 100 thin, bite-sized strips. Put the strips in a large, shallow dish. Mix together the soy, ginger and mustard, then add to the chicken and stir; cover. Leave for 1 hour.

2 Coat chicken strips in flour. Dip in beaten egg, then coat in breadcrumbs mixed with sesame seeds. Squeeze into torpedos.

3 Chill, spaced apart, for 1–2 hours to firm. Heat the oil in a deep-fat frier to 190°C (375°F). Deep-fry about 12 strips at a time for 5 minutes, turning them frequently to ensure they turn an even golden brown.

4 Drain on absorbent kitchen paper and keep hot in a low oven while frying the remainder. Serve hot.

CREAMY WATERCRESS QUICHE

| 0.55 | £ | ✳ | 404 cals |

Serves 6

shortcrust pastry made with 175 g
  (6 oz) flour (see recipe opposite)

50 g (2 oz) butter

1 large onion, skinned and chopped

1 bunch watercress, chopped

2 eggs

150 ml ($\frac{1}{4}$ pint) milk

150 ml (5 fl oz) single cream

salt and freshly ground pepper

1 Line a 20.5-cm (8-inch) flan
dish with the pastry. Place the
dish on a baking sheet. Bake blind
(see page 153).

2 Melt the butter in a saucepan,
add the onion and cook, stirring occasionally, for 3 minutes
until soft. Add the watercress, reserving a sprig to garnish, and cook
for a further 3–4 minutes. Remove the pan from the heat and
set aside.

3 Whisk together the eggs, milk,
cream and seasoning. Stir in
the cooked watercress mixture and
pour into the flan case.

4 Bake in the oven at 190°C
(375°F) mark 5 for 35 minutes
or until set. Serve hot or warm.
Garnish with a sprig of watercress.

HOT CRAB AND RICOTTA QUICHE

| 1.00 | £ £ | 421 cals |

Serves 6

175 g (6 oz) plain flour

salt and freshly ground pepper

40 g ($1\frac{1}{2}$ oz) butter or block
  margarine

40 g ($1\frac{1}{2}$ oz) lard

30 ml (2 tbsp) water

2 eggs

150 ml (5 fl oz) single cream

150 ml ($\frac{1}{4}$ pint) milk

225 g (8 oz) crab meat

175 g (6 oz) Ricotta cheese

30 ml (2 tbsp) grated Parmesan

1 Make the pastry. Mix the flour
and a pinch of salt together in a
bowl. Rub in the fats until the mixture resembles fine breadcrumbs.

2 Bind to a firm dough with the
cold water. Roll out on a lightly
floured surface and use to line
six 8.5-cm ($3\frac{1}{2}$-inch) fluted loose-
bottomed flan tins or a 20.5-cm
(8-inch) flan dish placed on a
baking sheet. Bake blind (see page
153) in the oven at 200°C (400°F)
mark 6 for 10–15 minutes.

3 Whisk the eggs, milk and cream
together in a bowl. Flake the
crabmeat, crumble the Ricotta and
add to the egg mixture with the
Parmesan and plenty of seasoning.
Pour into flan cases and bake in
the oven at 190°C (375°F) mark 5
for 35 minutes until golden.

SALATA PIZZAIOLA

0.15* £ 380 cals

* plus 1 hour refrigeration

Serves 6

450 g (1 lb) tomatoes, skinned and
    thinly sliced

150 ml ($\frac{1}{4}$ pint) olive oil

45–60 ml (3–4 tbsp) red wine
    vinegar

30 ml (2 tbsp) chopped fresh basil

salt and freshly ground pepper

1.25 ml ($\frac{1}{4}$ tsp) sugar

175 g (6 oz) sliced Italian salami

175 g (6 oz) Fontina or Mozzarella
    cheese

two 50-g (2-oz) cans anchovies in
    oil, drained and soaked in milk
    20 minutes

115-g (4-oz) can mussels, drained

1 Arrange the tomato slices, overlapping, on a flat, circular serving platter. Whisk together the oil,
45 ml (3 tbsp) vinegar, half the
basil and salt and pepper to taste.
Add more vinegar if liked. Sprinkle
the tomatoes evenly with the sugar,
then pour over half the dressing.

2 Cut the salami into thin strips,
removing the skin. Arrange a
section of salami on top of the
tomatoes, forming a pie-shaped
edge radiating out from centre.

3 Cut the cheese into strips and
arrange in the same way next
to the salami. Place the mussels
next to the cheese.

4 Repeat these sections of salami,
cheese and mussels until they
meet the first section of salami.
Drain the anchovies and pat dry.
Use lines of anchovies to separate
the different toppings.

5 Drizzle over the remaining
dressing, then refrigerate for
2–3 hours. Sprinkle with the remaining basil just before serving.

THREE-CHEESE LASAGNE

| 1.30 | £ | ✳ | 520 cals |

Serves 10

397-g (14-oz) can tomatoes
small onion, skinned and chopped
celery stick, trimmed and chopped
garlic clove, skinned and crushed
bay leaf
salt and freshly ground pepper
450 g (1 lb) minced beef
1 egg
50 g (2 oz) Parmesan cheese, grated
75 g (3 oz) plain flour
60 ml (4 tbsp) olive or vegetable oil
75 g (3 oz) butter or margarine
750 ml (1¼ pints) milk
100 g (4 oz) mild cured ham,
    chopped
100 g (4 oz) Mozzarella cheese,
    thinly sliced
100 g (4 oz) Bel Paese cheese, cut
    into strips
150 ml (5 fl oz) single cream
400 g (14 oz) lasagne

1 Prepare the tomato sauce by placing the tomatoes, onion, celery, garlic and bay leaf in a small pan, bring to the boil and simmer, uncovered, for 30 minutes. Stir occasionally to prevent sticking.

2 Discard the bay leaf and rub mixture through a sieve or purée in a blender. Season. Combine beef, egg, half the Parmesan and seasoning. Shape the mixture into twenty-four meatballs. Roll lightly in a little seasoned flour.

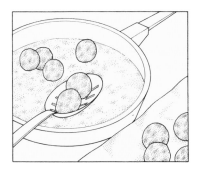

3 Heat the oil in a pan and cook the meatballs for about 5 minutes until brown. Remove with slotted spoon and drain.

4 Melt the butter in a pan, add in 65 g (2½ oz) flour and stirring, cook gently for 1 minute. Remove from the heat and gradually stir in the milk.

5 Bring to the boil and cook, stirring all the time, until the sauce thickens. Stir in the ham, Mozzarella, Bel Paese, cream and seasoning.

6 Prepare the lasagne as directed on the packet. In a large, greased, oval or rectangular oven-proof dish, layer up the lasagne, meatballs, tomato and white sauces, finishing with a layer of lasagne topped with white sauce.

7 Sprinkle over the remaining Parmesan cheese, then bake in the oven at 200°C (400°F) mark 6 for 20–25 minutes until golden brown.

FRESH CHERRY AND LEMON CHEESECAKE

| 0.30* | 🍴 | £ | 492 cals |

* plus 2–3 hours refrigeration

Serves 10

75 g (3 oz) butter

125 g (4 oz) caster sugar

150 g (5 oz) plain flour

egg yolk

225 g (8 oz) full fat soft cheese

225 g (8 oz) cottage cheese, sieved

2 eggs, separated

2 juicy lemons

142 ml (5 fl oz) soured cream

300 ml (10 fl oz) double cream

15 ml (1 tbsp) gelatine

45 ml (3 tbsp) water

225 g (8 oz) fresh red cherries, halved and stoned, or 213-g (7½-oz) can cherries, drained

angelica, to decorate

1 Cream butter with 75 g (3 oz) sugar. Mix to a firm dough with the flour and egg yolk. Roll out half to fit the base of a 20.5-cm (8-inch) spring release cake tin, and the other half to fit a 20.5-cm (8-inch) plain flan ring.

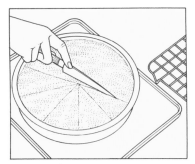

2 Bake both in the oven at 180°C (350°F) mark 4 for about 15 minutes. Cut the flan ring round into ten wedges and cool on a wire rack. Leave other round in tin.

3 With an electric mixer beat together the cheeses, 2 egg yolks, finely grated rind of the lemons, 75 ml (5 tbsp) lemon juice, remaining sugar and soured cream. Stir in half the double cream.

4 Soak the gelatine in water and dissolve, stir into cheese mixture. Refrigerate for 2–3 hours until beginning to set.

5 Whisk the egg whites until stiff. Fold cherries and egg whites into cheese mixture, turn into tin, refrigerate. Cover when firm.

6 Unmould. Place pastry wedges on top and decorate the cheesecake with angelica and the remaining double cream.

FULL FAT SOFT CHEESE AND COTTAGE CHEESE

Full fat soft cheese and cottage cheese are the two main ingredients of this cheesecake recipe, and you may wonder if it is necessary to use both. Full fat cream cheese contains 47.4 grammes of fat per 100 grammes of cheese, whereas cottage cheese contains only 4 grammes per 100 grammes. The recipe *can* be made with all full fat soft cheese if you like, but this will give a heavier result.

BOODLE'S ORANGE FOOL

2.10* f 332 cals

* includes 2 hours refrigeration

Serves 6

4–6 trifle sponge cakes, cut into 1-cm (½-inch) thick slices

grated rind and juice of 2 oranges

grated rind and juice of 1 lemon

25–50 g (1–2 oz) sugar

300 ml (10 fl oz) double cream

orange slices or segments, to decorate

1 Use the sponge cake slices to line the bottom and halfway up the sides of a deep dish or bowl.

2 Mix the orange and lemon rinds and juice with the sugar and stir until the sugar has completely dissolved.

3 In another bowl whip the cream until it just starts to thicken, then slowly add the sweetened fruit juice, continuing to whip the cream as you do so. Whip until the cream is light and thickened and the juice all absorbed.

4 Pour the mixture over the sponge cakes and refrigerate for at least 2 hours, longer if possible, so that the juice can permeate the sponge cakes and the cream thicken. Decorate with segments or slices of fresh orange.

BOODLE'S CLUB
This delicious orange fool has been a speciality for years at Boodle's Club in St James's Street, London, which was founded in 1764. It is so popular with the members of the club that the chef dares not take it off the menu! And many of the members are so fond of it that they've taken the recipe home with them – for their wives to make. This is our version.

MAIN COURSES

Poultry and Game

Poultry and game make a good choice for the main course of a dinner party – the quality of chicken, turkey, duck and game birds is extremely high, and it is rare that you will have to worry about the tenderness of the meat.

CHICKEN SUPREMES IN WINE AND CREAM

| 1.00 | £ £ | 411 cals |

45 ml (3 tbsp) red wine vinegar

50 g (2 oz) unsalted butter

6 French-style chicken supremes (with the wing bone attached), about 175 g (6 oz) each, wiped and trimmed of excess skin

1 small onion, skinned and roughly chopped

225 g (8 oz) tomatoes, skinned and roughly chopped

15 ml (1 tsp) tomato purée

1 large garlic clove, skinned and crushed

150 ml ($\frac{1}{4}$ pint) dry white wine

300 ml ($\frac{1}{2}$ pint) chicken stock

salt and freshly ground pepper

150 ml (5 fl oz) double cream

chopped fresh parsley, to garnish

1 Place the vinegar in a small saucepan and boil to reduce by half. Heat the butter in a large sauté or deep frying pan. Add the chicken pieces and brown well on all sides. Remove from the pan with a slotted spoon.

2 Add the onion, tomatoes, tomato purée and crushed garlic, cover and cook gently for about 5 minutes.

3 Add the wine and cook, uncovered, over a high heat for 5–10 minutes until the wine reduces by half. Add the vinegar, stock and seasoning and bring to the boil.

4 Replace the chicken, covering it with the sauce. Simmer gently, covered, for about 25 minutes or until the chicken is quite tender. Lift the chicken out of the pan with a slotted spoon and keep warm.

5 Boil the sauce until it is reduced by half, then stir in the cream. Continue reducing the sauce until a thin pouring consistency is obtained.

6 Adjust the seasoning, pass the sauce through a strainer and spoon over the chicken for serving. Garnish with chopped parsley.

Menu Suggestion
Serve with Avocado and Kiwi Fruit Vinaigrette (page 125) and Raspberry Pavlova (page 90).

——————— VARIATION ———————

Chicken breast fillets can be used instead of the French-style chicken supremes and, when in season, **75 g (3 oz) shallots** substituted for the onion.

Buying poultry
When buying fresh or chilled (non-frozen) chickens, feel the tip of the breast-bone with the thumb and finger. In a young bird this is soft and flexible; if it is hard and rigid the bird is probably too old to roast satisfactorily and will have to be steamed or boiled. Look at the feet also – in a young bird they are smooth with small (not coarse) scales and with short spurs.

DUCKLING ROULADES WITH PEACHES

| 2.00 | 🍴 🍴 £ £ ✳* | 742 cals |

6 duckling wing portions, about 350 g (12 oz) each

slices of onion and carrot, for flavouring

bay leaf

salt and freshly ground pepper

small onion, skinned and finely chopped

25 g (1 oz) hazelnuts, roughly chopped

2 firm, ripe peaches, skinned and chopped

65 g (2½ oz) butter

30 ml (2 tbsp) brandy

50 g (2 oz) fresh brown breadcrumbs

30 ml (2 tbsp) plain flour

bay leaves and peach slices, to garnish

1 Using a small sharp knife, carefully ease the skin and fat together off each of the six duckling wing portions.

2 Carefully fillet the duckling flesh in one piece away from the breastbone. Place the breast meat between sheets of cling film and bat out thinly with a meat mallet or rolling pin; cover and refrigerate until required. Cut any remaining duckling flesh off the wing bones. Chop finely and set aside until required.

3 To make the stock, place the wing bones in a saucepan together with the slices of onion and carrot, bay leaf and seasoning. Just cover with water and bring to the boil.

4 Simmer, uncovered, for 30–40 minutes or until about 300 ml (½ pint) stock remains. Strain off the stock and reserve.

5 Meanwhile, make the stuffing. Melt 25 g (1 oz) butter and fry the onion, chopped duckling flesh and hazelnuts for 3–4 minutes, turning frequently.

6 Stir in the peaches and fry for a few minutes longer or until the peaches are beginning to soften. Remove from the heat, stir in the brandy, breadcrumbs and seasoning, and cool.

7 Divide the cold stuffing between the duckling fillets and roll them up tightly. Secure each one with two wooden cocktail sticks. Sprinkle the flour over the rolls.

8 Melt the remaining butter in a large shallow flameproof casserole. Add the duckling rolls and brown lightly all over. Sprinkle in any remaining flour and then pour in 300 ml (½ pint) duckling stock. Season.

9 Bring to the boil, cover and bake in the oven at 180°C (350°F) mark 4 for about 40 minutes. Adjust seasoning and skim the juices before serving, garnished with peach slices and bay leaves.

Menu Suggestion
Serve with Avocado with Parma Ham (page 10) and Almond and Coffee Meringue Cake (page 107).

Buying duckling
Duckling portions can be found in most supermarkets and many butchers' shops. Alternatively, you could joint three duckling yourself, using the breast portions for this recipe and the legs for a pâté or casserole. Bat out the flesh thinly otherwise it's hard to make neat roulades.

CHICKEN WITH TARRAGON MAYONNAISE

1.50* £ £	645 cals

* plus 3–4 hours marinating

6 chicken leg joints

2 sticks of celery, washed, trimmed and sliced

200 ml (7 fl oz) medium dry white wine

30 ml (2 tbsp) chopped fresh tarragon or 10 ml (2 tsp) dried

salt and freshly ground pepper

300 ml ($\frac{1}{2}$ pint) mayonnaise (see page 155)

fresh tarragon sprigs or slices of lemon, to garnish

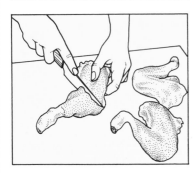

1 Skin the chicken leg joints and divide each one into a leg and thigh portion, making sure to trim away any excess fat.

2 Place the joints in a shallow ovenproof dish into which they will just fit. Scatter the celery over the chicken.

3 To make the marinade, mix the wine, chopped tarragon and seasoning together. Pour the marinade over the chicken.

4 Cover the dish and leave the chicken to marinate in a cool place for 3–4 hours, turning once. Cook, covered, in the oven at 180°C (350°F) mark 4 for about 1$\frac{1}{4}$ hours, or until chicken is tender.

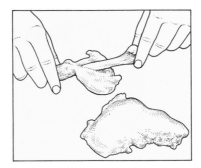

5 Leave the chicken to cool, covered. Strain off the cooking liquid and boil down until only 90 ml (6 tbsp) remains. Cool and set aside. Ease the bones out of the chicken pieces and arrange the joints on a serving plate.

6 Stir the reduced cooking liquid into the mayonnaise and spoon over the chicken just before serving. Garnish with fresh tarragon sprigs or lemon slices.

Menu Suggestion
Serve with Duck Pâté en Croûte Bigarade (page 18) and Individual Chocolate Mousses (page 113).

─── VARIATION ───

Chicken breasts can be used instead of leg joints and when fresh tarragon is not in season use **slices of fresh lemon** to garnish.

PHEASANT AU PORTO

| 1.50 | £ £ ✳ | 378 cals |

30 ml (2 tbsp) vegetable oil

3 young pheasants, well wiped

300 ml ($\frac{1}{2}$ pint) chicken stock

120 ml (8 tbsp) port

finely grated rind and juice of
2 oranges

50 g (2 oz) sultanas

salt and freshly ground pepper

20 ml (4 tsp) cornflour

25 g (1 oz) flaked almonds, toasted,
to garnish

1 Heat the oil in a large flameproof casserole. When hot, add
the pheasants and brown all over.

2 Pour the stock and port over
the birds. Add the orange rind
and juice with the sultanas and
season well. Bring to the boil.
Cover tightly and cook in the oven
at 170°C (325°F) mark 3 for 1–1$\frac{1}{2}$
hours.

3 Remove the birds from the
casserole, then joint each
pheasant into two or three pieces,
depending on size, and arrange on
a serving dish; keep warm.

4 Boil up juices with cornflour
mixed to a smooth paste with a
little water, stirring. Adjust
seasoning and spoon over
pheasant. Garnish with toasted
flaked almonds.

Menu Suggestion
Serve with Chestnut and Orange
Soup (page 9) and Individual
Chocolate Mousses (page 113).

MARINATED TURKEY WITH ASPARAGUS

| 0.50* | 🍴 🍴 | £ £ | 433 cals |

* plus 3–4 hours marinating

900 g (2 lb) turkey fillets

900 ml (1½ pints) chicken stock

salt and freshly ground pepper

30 ml (2 tbsp) chopped fresh parsley

50 g (2 oz) walnuts, chopped

1 garlic clove, skinned and crushed

20 ml (4 tsp) ground ginger

450 ml (¾ pint) French dressing (see page 155)

450 g (1 lb) fresh asparagus, scraped and trimmed

5 ml (1 tsp) salt

celery leaves, to garnish

1 Put the turkey fillets in a large saucepan and add enough well-seasoned chicken stock to cover. Poach for about 20 minutes until tender. Leave to cool in the liquid.

2 Meanwhile, make the marinade. Stir the parsley, walnuts, crushed garlic and ginger into the French dressing.

3 Tie the asparagus stalks into two neat bundles. Wedge upright in a large deep saucepan, cover tips with foil.

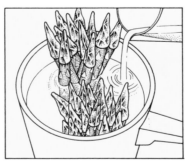

4 Pour in enough boiling water to come three-quarters of the way up the asparagus stalks. Add salt, return to the boil and simmer gently for about 10 minutes.

5 Lift the bundles carefully out of the water, place in a dish and remove the string. While still hot, stir in half the dressing. Leave the asparagus to cool.

6 Cut the turkey into 0.5 cm (¼ inch) wide strips. Marinate in the remaining dressing for 3–4 hours.

7 To serve, arrange the turkey strips and asparagus in a serving dish. Garnish with celery leaves. Serve chilled.

Menu Suggestion
Serve with Smoked Salmon and Trout Mousse (page 20) and Pineapple Cheesecake (page 120).

PREPARING AND COOKING ASPARAGUS
Asparagus is a delicate vegetable and needs careful preparation. Rinse each stalk very gently to wash away any dirt. Scrape or shave the length of each stalk, starting just below the tip. Cut off any ends if they are very woody (don't throw them away, they can be used in soup for extra flavour). Trim the stalks to roughly the same length and tie them into neat bundles of six to eight stalks of an even thickness (heads all at one end). Secure each bundle under the tips and near the base.

Cook asparagus with care. Use a special asparagus pan or wedge bundles upright in a deep saucepan containing enough boiling salted water to come three-quarters of the way up the stalks. Cover the tips with foil and simmer gently for about 10 minutes, until tender. This way the stalks are poached while the delicate tips are gently steamed.

BONED STUFFED POUSSINS

| 2.05 | 🗎 🗎 f f | 695 cals |

3 double poussins, about 700 g
    (1½ lb each)

2 large onions, skinned

carrot, peeled

bay leaf

6 black peppercorns

salt

125 g (4 oz) butter or margarine

175 g (6 oz) mixed nuts, chopped

two 227-g (8-oz) packets frozen
    chopped spinach, thawed

175 g (6 oz) fresh white
    breadcrumbs

grated rind and juice of 1 lemon

2 eggs, size 6, beaten

freshly ground pepper

150 ml (¼ pint) dry white wine

15 ml (1 tbsp) cornflour

dash of gravy browning

watercress, to garnish

1 Rinse the poussins under cold running water making sure that any blood is cleaned away, and pat the cavities dry with absorbent kitchen paper.

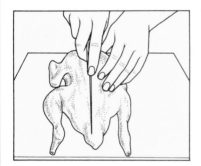

2 Place the poussins breast side down on a chopping board. Using a sharp knife, cut along the backbone.

3 With a small knife, ease flesh and skin away from bone, keeping knife close to backbone and ribcage.

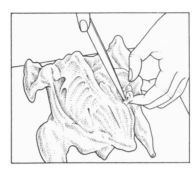

4 On reaching the joints, push the knife into them and ease them open.

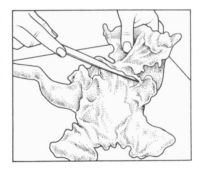

5 Continue to ease the flesh off the bone until the breast-bone is reached. Carefully separate the flesh and carcass.

6 To make the stock, place the bones, one onion, quartered, the carrot, bay leaf, peppercorns and a little salt in a pan. Add 1 litre (1¾ pints) water, bring to the boil, then simmer uncovered for about 30 minutes. Strain and reserve the stock. There should be about 568 ml (1 pint).

7 Meanwhile, make the stuffing. Chop the remaining onion finely. Heat 50 g (2 oz) butter in a pan, fry the onion and nuts for 2–3 minutes, then add the spinach and stir over a high heat. Cool slightly, then add the bread-crumbs, lemon rind and juice, egg to bind, and seasoning.

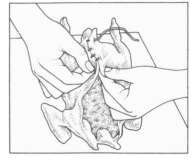

8 Lay the birds flesh side up and divide the stuffing between them. Fold skin over and sew up with cotton.

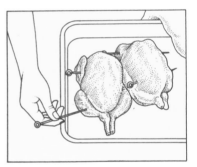

9 Push a skewer through the leg and wing joints and tie the knuckle ends together.

10 Place in a large roasting tin and spread over the remaining butter. Pour over half the stock and the wine. Roast in the oven at 200°C (400°F) mark 6 for 1 hour.

11 Put birds on a large board, remove skewers and string and cut each in half lengthwise. Place on warm serving dish.

12 Mix the cornflour with a little water; add to roasting tin with the stock. Cook for 2 minutes, stirring. Season, add browning and serve.

Menu Suggestion
Serve with Feta Cheese Soufflé (page 10) and Gooseberry Charlotte (page 110).

DUCKLING WITH BRANDY AND GREEN PEPPERCORN SAUCE

| 2.10 | 🛒 🛒 £ £ ✳ | 715 cals |

6 duckling portions

salt

3 large oranges

45 ml (3 tbsp) vegetable oil

1 onion, skinned and chopped

30 ml (2 tbsp) green peppercorns, lightly crushed

30 ml (2 tbsp) plain flour

300 ml (½ pint) chicken stock

freshly ground pepper

30 ml (2 tbsp) brandy

dash of gravy browning

1 Wipe the duckling portions all over and pat dry with absorbent kitchen paper; place on a wire rack over a roasting tin.

2 Prick the skin well with a fork and sprinkle with salt. Roast in the oven at 180°C (350°F) mark 4 for about 1 hour or until the juices run clear, basting occasionally.

3 Meanwhile, make the sauce. Remove the peel from one orange and cut it into fine shreds.

4 Blanch in boiling water for 1 minute. Drain. Squeeze out juice and reserve. Slice the remaining oranges.

5 Heat the oil in a medium saucepan, add the chopped onion and fry gently until golden.

6 Then stir in the lightly crushed peppercorns and flour and cook gently, stirring, for 1–2 minutes.

7 Blend in the stock with the orange juice. Season and bring to the boil, stirring all the time; simmer for about 4 minutes.

8 Separately, ignite the brandy and add to the sauce with a dash of gravy browning and a few orange shreds. Adjust seasoning.

9 Heat the sauce to boiling point and serve separately. Garnish the duck portions with orange slices and remaining shreds.

Menu Suggestion
Serve with Vegetable and Ham Terrine (page 71) and Boodle's Orange Fool (page 55).

GREEN PEPPERCORNS
Green peppercorns sold in cans are preserved in brine; fresh green peppercorns are available from the vegetable sections of some large supermarkets. Both are suitable for this recipe.

Green peppercorns are in fact the unripe berries of the *Piper nigrum* tree, from which come the more familiar white and green peppercorns. (White peppercorns are the fully ripened berries, black peppercorns come from the berries which were picked when green then left to dry in the sun.)

The fresh pungent flavour of green peppercorns is totally different from the dried varieties, and their unusual tang adds interest to most grilled meats and poultry; it goes especially well with duckling as it helps offset the natural richness of the meat.

Wedding Buffet for 50 People

AVOCADO MOUSSES

0.15*	£ £	535 cals

* plus 2–3 hours refrigeration

Makes 12 as a starter

4 ripe avocados, about 900 g (2 lb) total weight, peeled and stoned
2 onions, skinned and grated
1 egg, hard-boiled and chopped
2 garlic cloves, crushed
60 ml (4 tbsp) lemon juice
300 ml (10 fl oz) soured cream
600 ml (1 pint) mayonnaise
salt and freshly ground pepper
30 ml (2 tbsp) gelatine
60 ml (4 tbsp) water
3 egg whites
halved stuffed olives and endive, to garnish

1 Peel and stone the avocados. Press through a nylon sieve. Stir onion and egg into avocado with the garlic. Mix lemon juice, soured cream and mayonnaise and beat into avocado mixture. Season.

2 In a small bowl, sprinkle the gelatine over 60 ml (4 tbsp) water. Leave for 2–3 minutes. Heat gently over a pan of hot water until completely dissolved. Pour into the avocado mixture in a thin steady stream, beating all the time.

3 Whisk egg whites until stiff; fold into avocado mixture. Adjust seasoning. Spoon into individual serving dishes (about 175 ml [6 fl oz] each).

4 Cover with cling film, chill for 2–3 hours, then serve garnished with stuffed olives and endive.

VEGETABLE AND HAM TERRINE

| 2.00* | 🟦 | £ | 397 cals |

* plus overnight refrigeration

Serves 10 as a starter

| about 30 young spinach leaves |
| 3 large carrots |
| 2 red peppers |
| 350 g (12 oz) French beans |
| 450 g (1 lb) full fat soft cheese |
| 450 g (1 lb) boiled ham |
| 1.25 ml ($\frac{1}{4}$ tsp) Tabasco sauce |
| freshly ground pepper to taste |
| 2 egg whites |

1 Remove large stalks from spinach. Blanch leaves in boiling water for 10 seconds. Drain and dry; reserve water.

2 Line the base and sides of a 1-kg (2-lb) loaf tin with the spinach leaves, making sure there are no gaps. Reserve five leaves.

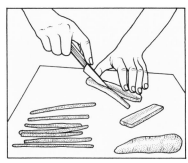

3 Using a vegetable peeler, peel the carrots, then cut them lengthways into matchsticks.

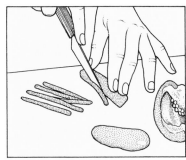

4 Cut the peppers in half, then remove the core and seeds and slice the flesh into thin strips. Top and tail the beans.

5 Blanch the prepared vegetables in the spinach water. Allow 2 minutes blanching time for each type of vegetable.

6 Put the cheese in a food processor. Tear the ham into shreds, add to the cheese with the Tabasco, pepper and egg whites. Work to a smooth mixture.

7 Divide the cheese and ham mixture into five even-sized pieces so that terrine looks even.

8 Put a portion of the cheese and ham mixture in the bottom of the tin, spreading it out evenly. Top with half the beans, placing them lengthways and close together.

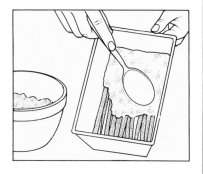

9 Cover the beans with another portion of cheese and ham, then with the carrots, placing them lengthways as the beans. Top with another layer of cheese and ham, then a layer of red pepper strips.

10 Repeat cheese and ham layer, then beans and another cheese layer. Finish with layer of reserved spinach. Cover with foil.

11 Bake the terrine in a hot bain marie in the oven at 180°C (350°F) mark 4 for 1$\frac{1}{2}$ hours. Remove and leave to cool. When completely cold, refrigerate overnight. To serve, turn the terrine out on to an oblong plate or board. Serve sliced.

CHICKEN GALANTINE

2.00* ⊔ ⊓ £ £ ✳* 244 cals

* plus 2–3 hours cooling time and 1
  hour setting time; freeze before
  adding aspic jelly.

Makes 15 small buffet portions

| 1.4 kg (3 lb) chicken, with giblets |
| 2 onions, skinned |
| 50 g (2 oz) mushrooms |
| 50 g (2 oz) butter |
| finely grated rind and juice of 1 lemon |
| 10 ml (2 tsp) ground coriander |
| 1 garlic clove, skinned and crushed |
| 450 g (1 lb) pork sausagemeat |
| 1 egg, beaten |
| salt and freshly ground pepper |
| 50 g (2 oz) sliced tongue |
| 50 g (2 oz) sliced ham |
| about 300 ml ($\frac{1}{2}$ pint) liquid aspic jelly |
| cucumber, olives, tarragon and hard-boiled egg, to garnish |

1 Bone the chicken (see page
158). (Alternatively, you can
ask your butcher to do this for
you.) Reserve the liver.

2 Prepare the stuffing. Finely
chop the onions, mushrooms
and liver. Sauté in the butter with
the lemon rind, coriander and
garlic, until softened. Stir in 30 ml
(2 tbsp) lemon juice. Cool. Mix
with sausagemeat and egg. Season.

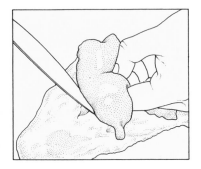

3 Lay the chicken out, with its
flesh side uppermost. Remove
breast fillets with a knife.

4 Place half the stuffing over the
centre of the bird. Cover with
the tongue. Add the fillets, cover
with the ham and then finish with
the remaining stuffing.

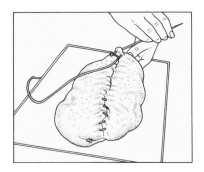

5 Sew up the chicken into a neat
shape. Wrap tightly in a double
layer of muslin. Secure well, sew-
ing up the join. Place in a large
pan with just enough boiling water
to cover.

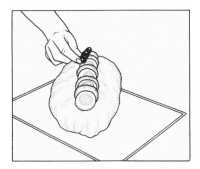

6 Bring to the boil, cover and
simmer for 1$\frac{1}{2}$ hours. Lift from
the pan. Cool for 2–3 hours. When
cold, remove cloth and string.
Make the aspic jelly and use to
coat the chicken. Garnish. Cover
with more aspic. Leave to set for
about 2 hours, and serve sliced.

POACHED SALMON

| 0.35* | £ £ | 190 cals |

* plus 3 hours cooling and 1½ hours setting time

Makes 15 small buffet portions

1 small salmon, about 1.8 kg (4 lb)

150 ml (¼ pint) dry white wine

slices of onion

bay leaf

salt and freshly ground pepper

300 ml (½ pint) liquid aspic jelly

lemon slices, cucumber, black olives, whole prawns and endive, to garnish

mayonnaise, to serve

1 Rinse the fish, remove eyes and trim tail and fins. Place in a fish kettle. Pour over wine and enough water to just cover fish. Add onion, bay leaf, salt and pepper. Bring slowly to the boil, cover and simmer for 25 minutes.

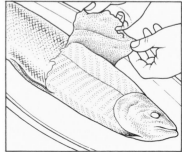

2 Lift out of liquor; cool for 2–3 hours. Ease off skin. Place fish on serving platter.

3 As the aspic begins to set, brush some over the fish. Leave to set for 1–1½ hours. Coat with several layers of aspic.

4 Garnish with slices of lemon, cucumber skin and olives. Brush more aspic on top. Arrange endive, whole prawns and sliced cucumber and lemon on side of dish and serve with mayonnaise.

EXOTIC FRUIT SALAD

0.15* £ £ ✳ 75 cals

*plus 2–3 hours chilling time

Serves 10

1 medium pineapple

1 mango

1 papaya (optional)

3 nectarines

100 g (4 oz) black or green grapes

1 ogen melon, halved and seeded

juice of 3 large oranges

juice of 1 lemon

45 ml (3 tbsp) orange liqueur

fresh mint sprigs, to decorate

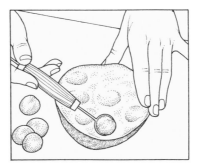

4 With a melon baller scoop out melon flesh into dish. Scrape out remaining flesh, chop and add to the serving dish.

5 Mix together the orange juice, lemon juice and liqueur. Pour over the fruit and chill for 2–3 hours. Decorate with mint.

1 Cut the pineapple into 1 cm (½ inch) slices. Remove skin and cut flesh into cubes. Place in dish.

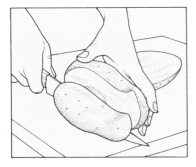

2 Cut a chunk off each side of the mango lengthways to expose the stone. Ease off the flesh. Remove outer skin and slice flesh thinly. Add to dish. Repeat with papaya and add to dish.

3 Wash nectarines and slice flesh away from stone. Add to dish with halved and seeded grapes.

STRAWBERRY AND KIWI FRUIT FLAN

| 0.35* | £ £ | 303 cals |

* plus 1 hour cooling time

Serves 10

454 g (1 lb) packet frozen puff
   pastry, thawed, or 225 g (8 oz)
   homemade (page 152)

beaten egg

340-g (12-oz) jar apricot jam

30 ml (2 tbsp) lemon juice

450 g (1 lb) fresh strawberries

3 medium kiwi fruit

1 Roll out three-quarters of the pastry to a 30.5-cm (12-inch) round. Place the dough on a baking sheet and prick well all over. Make sure you do not puncture the base of the pastry round.

2 Using a 7.5-cm (3-inch) fluted cutter, stamp out eight to ten crescents from the pastry dough which remains.

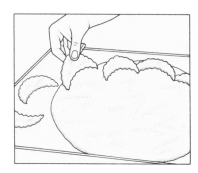

3 Brush the pastry round with beaten egg and arrange the crescents around the edge; brush these with egg, too.

4 Bake the pastry case in the oven at 220°C (425°F) mark 7 for 12 minutes. Prick the base again, then lower the heat to 170°C (325°F) mark 3 for a further 10 minutes; remove from oven and leave to cool for 1 hour.

5 Warm the apricot jam and lemon juice, sieve and return to the pan. Brush a little over the base of the pastry case.

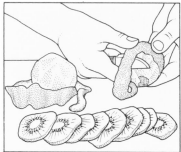

6 Hull the strawberries, peel and slice the kiwi fruit. Arrange the fruit in wedge shapes in the pastry case, radiating outwards from the centre to the pastry crescents.

7 Using the pastry brush, glaze the fruit and pastry edge with remaining jam.

MAIN COURSES

Fish and Shellfish

For a light main course for a dinner party – particularly in summer – fish and shellfish are a wise choice, and you will find that your guests welcome a change from the more usual main course dishes of meat, poultry and game.

BAKED TROUT WITH LEMON

1.20*	£	582 cals

* plus 2 hours standing time

6 medium rainbow trout, gutted
115 g (4½ oz) butter
90 ml (6 tbsp) lemon juice
90 ml (6 tbsp) chopped parsley
salt and freshly ground pepper
25 g (1 oz) almonds, chopped
grated rind of 1 lemon
100 g (4 oz) fresh breadcrumbs
1 egg, beaten
45 ml (3 tbsp) plain flour
300 ml (½ pint) fish stock
2 egg yolks
90 ml (6 tbsp) double cream
lemon slices and fennel tops, to
garnish

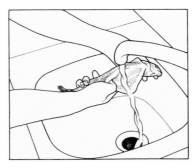

1 Wash each of the trout well under cold running water, ensuring that all blood clots under backbone are removed. Pat dry.

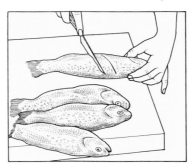

2 Make three or four diagonal slashes about 0.5 cm (¼ inch) deep on either side of each fish. Place the fish, side by side, in a shallow, ovenproof dish.

3 Melt 75 g (3 oz) butter in a small saucepan. Leave to cool, then mix in the lemon juice, 75 ml (5 tbsp) parsley and seasoning and pour over the fish. Cover with cling film and leave in a cool place (not the refrigerator) for 2 hours, turning and basting once.

4 Meanwhile, make the stuffing. Mix together the almonds, grated lemon rind, breadcrumbs, seasoning, remaining parsley and egg to bind.

5 Remove the cling film from the dish and fill the cavities of the fish with the stuffing. Cover the dish with foil and bake in the oven at 180°C (350°F) mark 4 for about 40 minutes.

6 Meanwhile, make the sauce. Melt the remaining 40 g (1½ oz) butter in a small saucepan. Add the flour and cook for 1–2 minutes, stirring. Remove from the heat and gradually stir in the stock. Bring to the boil, reduce the heat and continue to cook, stirring all the time until the sauce thickens.

7 Remove from the heat. Blend the egg yolks with the cream and stir into the sauce. Season with salt and pepper. Remove the foil from the fish and stir the cooking juices into the sauce. Reheat gently without boiling.

8 Pour some of the sauce at side of fish, garnish with lemon slices and fennel tops and serve the remaining sauce separately.

Menu Suggestion
Serve with Almond Cream Soup (page 13) and Fresh Pear Short-cake (page 118).

BOUILLABAISSE

0.40 £ ✳ 432 cals

900 g (2 lb) fillets of mixed white
   fish and shellfish such as
   whiting, conger eel, monkfish
   and prawns

2–3 onions, skinned and sliced

1 stick of celery, washed and
   chopped

150 ml (¼ pint) olive oil

225 g (8 oz) tomatoes

pared rind of 1 orange

2 garlic cloves, crushed

bay leaf

2.5 ml (½ tsp) dried thyme

few parsley sprigs

salt and freshly ground pepper

pinch of saffron strands

whole prawns, to garnish

1 Wash the fish and pat it dry
   with absorbent kitchen paper.
Remove any skin, then cut fish
into fairly large, thick pieces.

2 Lightly fry the sliced onions
   and chopped celery in the oil
in a large, heavy-based saucepan
for 5 minutes or until soft. Skin
and slice the tomatoes.

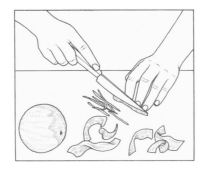

3 Finely shred the orange rind,
   then stir half into the onion
and celery with the garlic, herbs,
salt and pepper. Dissolve the
saffron in a little hot water.

4 Put the fish in with the
   vegetables. Add the saffron
water and just enough cold water
to cover. Bring to the boil and
simmer, uncovered, for 8 minutes.

5 Add the prawns and cook for a
   further 5–8 minutes. Garnish
with prawns and remaining orange
rind.

Menu Suggestion
Serve with Stuffed Globe Arti-
chokes (page 14) and Mango Ice
Cream (page 112).

USING SAFFRON
Saffron strands are the dried
stigma of the autumn flowering
crocus. Although they are very
expensive to buy (saffron is the
most expensive spice in the
world), always use them in recipes like this one which calls
for saffron water.

HOT FISH TERRINE WITH GRUYÈRE SAUCE

| 2.15 | £ £ | 549 cals |

75 g (3 oz) butter

1 garlic clove, skinned and crushed

60 ml (4 tbsp) plain flour

750 ml (1¼ pints) milk

550 g (1¼ lb) hake fillets, skinned and chopped

150 ml (5 fl oz) double cream

10 ml (2 tsp) anchovy essence

3 eggs

1 egg yolk

salt and freshly ground pepper

30 ml (2 tbsp) chopped parsley

125 g (4 oz) shelled prawns, chopped

125 g (4 oz) Gruyère cheese, grated

watercress sprigs and 6 whole prawns, to garnish

1 Lightly butter and base line a 1.6-litre (2¾-pint) shallow loaf tin or terrine. Make sure not to use too much butter.

2 Melt 40 g (1½ oz) butter in a saucepan. Add garlic. Stir in 45 ml (3 tbsp) flour and cook for 2 minutes. Remove from the heat and gradually stir in 450 ml (¾ pint) milk. Bring to the boil, stirring. Simmer for 2 minutes.

3 In a blender or food processor, purée the sauce, raw chopped fish, cream, anchovy essence, eggs and yolk. Season lightly.

4 Spoon half the fish mixture into the tin. Sprinkle with parsley and half the prawns. Spoon in the rest of fish mixture. Cover tightly with buttered greaseproof paper.

5 Place in a roasting tin with hot water to come halfway up the sides of the terrine. Cook in the oven at 150°C (300°F) mark 2 for about 1¾ hours.

6 Just before the terrine is cooked, make the sauce. Melt 25 g (1 oz) butter in a pan. Stir in 15 ml (1 tbsp) flour and cook for 2 minutes.

7 Remove from the heat and gradually stir in the remaining milk. Bring to the boil, stirring. Simmer for 2 minutes. Off the heat, stir in the grated cheese and remaining prawns. Season to taste.

8 Invert the terrine on to a warm serving dish and tilt slightly to drain off juice. Remove cooking container. Spoon a little sauce over terrine and garnish with watercress and prawns. Serve the rest separately.

Menu Suggestion
Serve with Avocado with Parma Ham (page 10) and Raspberry and Apple Torte (page 115).

STUFFED PAUPIETTES OF SOLE

| 1.05 | f f | 482 cals |

18 lemon sole quarter-cut fillets (two from each side of fish)

75 g (3 oz) butter

½ onion, peeled and chopped

225 g (8 oz) button mushrooms, wiped and trimmed

75 g (3 oz) fresh white breadcrumbs

finely grated rind of 1 lemon

15 ml (1 tbsp) chopped fresh tarragon leaves

salt and freshly ground pepper

300 ml (½ pint) dry white wine

150 ml (¼ pint) water

30 ml (2 tbsp) plain flour

about 90 ml (6 tbsp) double cream, at room temperature

fresh tarragon sprigs, to garnish

1 Skin the fillets of sole. Hold each fillet flesh side uppermost at the tail end (dipping your fingers in a little salt helps grip the slippery skin).

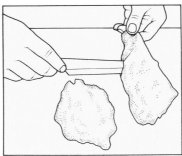

2 Using a sharp knife and a sawing action, work away from you to remove the skin. Wash fish.

3 Make the stuffing. Melt 25 g (1 oz) of the butter in a saucepan. Add the onion and fry gently until lightly coloured.

4 Meanwhile, slice half the mushrooms and chop the remainder very finely. Put the chopped mushrooms in a bowl with the breadcrumbs, lemon rind and tarragon.

5 Add the softened onion and season to taste; stir well until the mixture clings together.

6 Place a sole fillet, skinned side uppermost, on a board. Put a teaspoonful of stuffing on one end of fillet. Roll fish up around it. Secure with a cocktail stick.

7 Stand in an upright position in a well-buttered baking dish. Repeat with remaining sole fillets, placing them side by side in dish.

8 Mix together the wine and water and pour over the fish. Cover loosely with foil and bake in the oven at 190°C (375°F) mark 5 for 15 minutes.

9 Remove the fish from the cooking liquid with a slotted spoon and discard the cocktail sticks. Place the fish in a single layer in a warmed serving dish, cover and keep warm. Strain the liquid into a jug.

10 Melt 25 g (1 oz) butter in a saucepan, sprinkle in the flour and cook for 1–2 minutes, stirring. Remove from the heat then gradually stir in the strained cooking liquid. Bring to the boil, reduce the heat and simmer gently for 5 minutes, stirring until thick.

11 Meanwhile, melt the remaining butter in a frying pan, add the finely sliced mushrooms and fry gently.

12 Whisk the cream into the sauce. Pour a little sauce over each paupiette; then garnish with sliced mushrooms and tarragon sprigs. Pour any remaining sauce into a warmed sauceboat.

Menu Suggestion

Serve with Avocado and Kiwi Fruit Vinaigrette (page 125) and Melon and Ginger Sorbet (page 47).

MONKFISH AND MUSSEL BROCHETTES

0.40	£ £	365 cals

900 g (2 lb) monkfish, skinned and boned

36 mussels, cooked

18 rashers streaky bacon, rinded and halved

50 g (2 oz) butter, melted

60 ml (4 tbsp) chopped parsley

finely grated rind and juice of 1 lime or lemon

4 garlic cloves, skinned and crushed

salt and freshly ground pepper

shredded lettuce, bay leaves, and lime or lemon wedges, to garnish

1 Cut the fish into 42 cubes. Using a sharp knife, shell the mussels. Reserve the mussels and discard the shells.

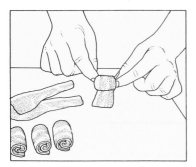

2 Roll the bacon rashers up neatly. Thread the cubed fish, mussels and bacon alternately on to six oiled kebab skewers.

3 Mix together the melted butter, parsley, lime rind and juice, garlic and salt and pepper to taste. (Take care when adding salt as both the mussels and the bacon are naturally salty.)

4 Place the brochettes on an oiled grill or barbecue rack. Brush with the butter mixture, then grill under a moderate grill for 15 minutes. Turn the brochettes frequently during cooking and brush with the butter mixture with each turn.

5 Arrange the hot brochettes on a serving platter lined with shredded lettuce. Garnish with bay leaves and lime wedges and serve at once with saffron rice, if liked.

Menu Suggestion
Serve with Mexican Avocado Dip (page 24) and Raspberry Pavlova (page 90).

PREPARING AND COOKING FRESH MUSSELS

When buying fresh mussels from the fishmonger, buy a good dozen more than you need to allow for those that are open. As soon as you get the mussels home, put them in a deep bowl of cold water and leave to soak for about 1 hour, changing the water several times. If any of the mussels are still open after this time, throw them away. Scrub the closed mussels clean with a stiff brush, scraping off any encrustations with a knife. Put them in a large pan with about 150 ml ($\frac{1}{4}$ pint) dry white wine or wine and water, garlic, herbs and seasoning to taste. Bring to the boil, then cover and simmer for 5–7 minutes until the shells open; discard any that do not.

MALAYSIAN-STYLE PRAWNS

0.25	£ £	394 cals

30 ml (2 tbsp) vegetable oil

1 onion, skinned and very finely chopped

2 garlic cloves, skinned and crushed

2.5-cm (1-inch) piece fresh root ginger, skinned and crushed

2 dried red chillis, finely chopped

15 ml (1 tbsp) ground coriander

10 ml (2 tsp) ground turmeric

5 ml (1 tsp) salt

700 g (1½ lb) peeled prawns

half a 200-g (7-oz) block creamed coconut, broken into pieces

about 300 ml (½ pint) boiling water

juice of 1 lime or lemon

15–25 g (½–1 oz) coconut shreds or shredded coconut (optional)

lime or lemon slices, whole prawns (optional) and fresh coriander sprigs, to garnish

1 Heat the oil in a wok or large frying pan, add the onion, garlic and ginger and fry gently for 5 minutes. Sprinkle in the chillis, spices and salt and stir-fry for 2–3 minutes more.

2 Add the prawns to the pan and stir-fry for 5 minutes until heated through and evenly coated in the spice mixture.

3 Crumble in the coconut, then gradually add the water and bring to the boil, stirring all the time (add just enough water to make a thick gravy that coats the prawns). Simmer for 5 minutes, stirring frequently. Taste and add salt, if necessary.

4 Transfer to a warmed serving dish and squeeze the juice from the lime evenly over the top. Sprinkle with the coconut shreds, if used, then garnish with lime or lemon slices, whole prawns, if used, and coriander. Serve immediately.

Menu Suggestion
Serve with Chilled Asparagus Soup (page 22) and Melon and Ginger Sorbet (page 47).

PRAWNS
Frozen peeled prawns can be used for this dish, but fresh prawns in their shells are usually larger, more succulent and flavoursome – even if they are fiddly and take a long time to prepare!

To cut down on cost, you can buy less prawns than specified in the recipe and make up the weight with button mushrooms. Wipe them and slice them neatly into 'T' shapes, then quickly toss them in a little butter and lemon juice. Drain them thoroughly with a slotted spoon, then add them at the end of step 2 and stir to combine with the prawns, just before you crumble in the coconut.

Barbecue Party for 10 People

ICED TZAZIKI SOUP

| 0.10* | £ | 51 cals |

* plus 2–3 hours chilling time
Serves 10

2 medium cucumbers, peeled
900 ml (1½ pints) natural yogurt
2 small garlic cloves, crushed
45 ml (3 tbsp) chopped fresh mint
750 ml (1¼ pints) chicken stock
salt and freshly ground pepper
mint leaves, to garnish

1 Wash the cucumber and pat dry with absorbent kitchen paper. Quarter the cucumber lengthways and discard the seeds, using a teaspoon.

2 Dice the cucumber finely, cutting up three or four strips at a time. Then place yogurt in a bowl and stir in cucumber, garlic and chopped mint.

3 Stir in the chicken stock and season. Place in the refrigerator for 2–3 hours to chill. Then serve, garnished with mint.

MUSTARD CHICKEN DRUMSTICKS

| 0.35 | £ | 125 cals |

Serves 10

50 g (2 oz) butter
45 ml (3 tbsp) coarse grain mustard
1 lemon
5 ml (1 tsp) chopped fresh tarragon or rosemary
salt and freshly ground pepper
10 chicken drumsticks
rosemary sprigs, to garnish

1 In a bowl, cream the butter until soft. Work in the mustard a little at a time using a wooden spoon. Grate in the lemon rind; gradually beat in 15 ml (1 tbsp) lemon juice and the herbs and seasoning.

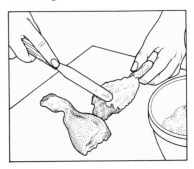

2 Spread the mustard butter over the chicken pieces, coating evenly. Chill in the refrigerator, if not cooking immediately.

3 Barbecue for 10–15 minutes on each side until the skin is crisp, golden and the chicken is tender. Keep back some of the mustard butter and spread on the chicken pieces as they cook.

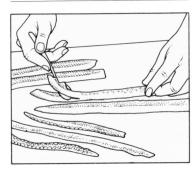

HONEY-GLAZED KEBABS

0.30*	350 cals*

* plus 4 hours marinating; calories
include pitta bread

Serves 10

1.1 kg (2½ lb) boned lean shoulder
  or leg of lamb

432-g (15¼-oz) can pineapple slices

75 ml (5 tbsp) clear honey

75 ml (5 tbsp) soy sauce

45 ml (3 tbsp) tomato ketchup

12.5 ml (2½ tsp) malt vinegar

2 large garlic cloves, crushed

5 small sprigs fresh rosemary

salt and freshly ground pepper

2 medium green peppers

275 g (10 oz) button mushrooms

pitta bread or large baps, to serve

1 Using a sharp knife, trim any
excess fat from the meat and
cut into 2.5-cm (1-inch) cubes.
Place in a bowl and set aside.

2 Drain the pineapple juice into
a small saucepan, adding the
honey, soy sauce, tomato ketchup,
vinegar, garlic, rosemary and
seasoning. Heat until the honey
melts; cool. Pour over meat, cover
and leave for at least 4 hours (in as
cool a place as possible).

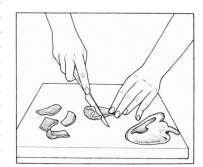

3 Halve and seed the peppers
and cut into bite-sized pieces.
Cut the pineapple slices into
similar-sized pieces.

4 Drain the lamb, reserve the
marinade and thread on to 20
skewers with the pineapple, pepper
and mushrooms.

5 Brush with the marinade and
barbecue for 15–20 minutes,
turning and basting frequently.
Serve pocketed in warmed pitta
bread or baps.

> **HONEY**
> Honey was the first sweetener
> known to man – the ancient
> Greeks and Romans were ad-
> dicted to it, long before sugar
> was ever heard of. Honey is made
> up of several different types
> of sugar – fructose and glucose
> being the major two – and it is
> known to be very nutritious. It is
> rich in vitamins B_1 and C, ribo-
> flavin and niacin, and minerals.

PINE NUT PILAFF

0.40	✳	252 cals

350 g (12 oz) Basmati rice

75 g (3 oz) butter

1 onion, skinned and chopped

2 large garlic cloves, skinned and
    finely chopped

8 cardamom pods, crushed

1.1 litres (2 pints) hot chicken stock

salt and freshly ground pepper

15 ml (1 tbsp) olive oil

100 g (4 oz) pine nuts

orange or yellow food colouring

50 g (2 oz) seedless raisins

fresh coriander, to garnish

1 Rinse the rice under cold running water. Drain well. Then melt 50 g (2 oz) of the butter in a large flameproof casserole. Add the onion and garlic and fry gently until soft and golden.

2 Add the rice and fry, stirring until the grains begin to burst. Add the cardamoms, then pour in the hot stock and bring to the boil. Add salt and pepper to taste and stir once. Lower the heat, cover and simmer gently for 15 minutes.

3 Meanwhile melt 15 g ($\frac{1}{2}$ oz) butter with the oil in a separate pan. Add the pine nuts and fry until golden brown, shaking the pan constantly. Drain on absorbent kitchen paper, turning occasionally.

4 Sprinkle a few drops of food colouring over the rice, cover again and simmer for a further 10 minutes until rice is tender.

5 Fork two-thirds of the pine nuts into the rice with the raisins and the remaining butter. Taste and adjust seasoning. Cover, turn off the heat and leave to stand for 5 minutes. Serve garnished with the remaining pine nuts and the coriander.

PIPERANA

| 0.30* | £ | 82 cals |

* plus overnight standing time

Serves 10

10 peppers (red, green and yellow)

4 large garlic cloves, skinned and crushed

5–10 ml (1–2 tsp) grated onion

150 ml ($\frac{1}{4}$ pint) olive oil

60 ml (4 tbsp) lemon juice

45 ml (3 tbsp) chopped fresh herbs (marjoram, thyme, parsley, etc.)

pinch of sugar, or to taste

salt and freshly ground pepper

1 Cook the peppers whole on the barbecue (or under the grill), turning them constantly until their skins are charred all over.

2 Remove from the heat, place in a bowl and immediately cover tightly with a damp, clean tea-towel. Leave until the peppers are cold, overnight if possible.

3 Hold the peppers over a bowl and rub the skins off with your fingers. Let the juices collect in the bowl. Discard skins. Tear the pepper flesh into long, thin shreds with your fingers, discarding stems, cores and seeds.

4 Put the garlic in a screw-top jar with the grated onion, oil, the lemon juice and reserved pepper juices. Add the herbs, with sugar and salt and pepper to taste. Shake well to mix.

5 Arrange the peppers decoratively on a plate. Pour over the dressing, then leave to stand for at least 10 minutes before serving.

RASPBERRY PAVLOVA

| 1.10* £ £ ✳* | 348 cals |

* plus 2 hours cooling time; freeze
  without topping

3 egg whites

175 g (6 oz) caster sugar

2.5 ml (½ tsp) vanilla flavouring

**2.5 ml (½ tsp) distilled white wine
vinegar**

5 ml (1 tsp) cornflour

300 ml (10 fl oz) double cream

**350 g (12 oz) fresh raspberries,
washed and hulled**

1 Draw an 18-cm (7-inch) circle
on a sheet of non-stick paper
and place the paper on a baking
sheet.

2 Whisk the egg whites until very
stiff. Whisk in half the sugar
then carefully fold in the remaining sugar, the vanilla flavouring,
white wine vinegar and cornflour
with a metal spoon.

3 Spread the meringue mixture
over the circle and bake in the
oven at 150°C (300°F) mark 2 for
about 1 hour until crisp and dry.
Leave to cool on the baking sheet
for 2 hours then carefully peel off
the non-stick paper.

4 Whisk the cream until stiff.
Slide the meringue on to a flat
plate, pile the cream on it and
arrange the raspberries on top.

BLACKCURRANT RIPPLE ICE CREAM

| 0.30* | £ | ✳ | 350 cals |

* plus 6–7 hours freezing time and
  30 minutes refrigeration

Serves 8

568 ml (1 pint) milk

1 vanilla pod

6 egg yolks

350 g (12 oz) sugar

600 ml (20 fl oz) whipping cream

450 g (1 lb) blackcurrants

120 ml (8 tbsp) water

1 Bring the milk and vanilla pod almost to the boil. Take off the heat, cover and leave to cool for at least 15 minutes.

2 Beat egg yolks and half the sugar together, stir in the milk and strain back into the pan. Cook the custard gently over a low heat. Do not boil.

3 Pour into a chilled, shallow container and leave to cool. Freeze for about 2 hours until mushy in texture around edges.

4 Turn into a large, chilled basin and mash with a flat whisk or fork. Whisk the cream until stiff and fold into the frozen mixture. Freeze for 2 hours until mushy.

5 Stalk and rinse the currants. Cook with the sugar and water until soft. Purée in blender and sieve to remove seeds. Cool.

6 Take the ice cream out of the freezer and whisk to a spreading consistency. Spoon a layer into freezer container. Pour over some of the blackcurrant purée. Continue to layer. Cover; return to freezer for 2 hours. To serve, allow to soften in the refrigerator for about 30 minutes.

Vegetables

Try not to be overambitious in your choice of vegetable dishes for a dinner party. It is far better to have one or two perfectly cooked vegetables than a wide selection of overcooked, soggy ones. If you choose a potato dish that can be cooked in the oven, this will leave you spare hands and cooker space to do a simple, quickly cooked vegetable dish just before serving the main course.

AUBERGINE GALETTE

2.00*	£	222 cals

* includes 30 minutes standing time

1.4 kg (3 lb) aubergines

salt

900 g (2 lb) fresh tomatoes, skinned and quartered, or two 397-g (14-oz) cans tomatoes, drained

30 ml (2 tbsp) tomato purée

1 garlic clove, skinned and crushed

50 ml (2 fl oz) olive oil, plus oil for frying and drizzling over cheese

5 ml (1 tsp) sugar

15 ml (1 tbsp) chopped fresh basil or 5 ml (1 tsp) dried

freshly ground pepper

200 g (7 oz) Mozzarella cheese, thinly sliced

50 g (2 oz) grated Parmesan cheese

fresh basil sprig, to garnish

1 Slice the aubergines into 0.5-cm (¼-inch) slices and place in a colander or large sieve. Sprinkle liberally with salt and set aside for 30 minutes to ensure that the bitter flavour is completely removed.

2 Meanwhile, make the tomato sauce. Place the tomatoes, tomato purée, garlic, olive oil, sugar and basil together in a pan. Stir well and simmer gently for 20 minutes until the liquid is reduced by half. Season with salt and freshly ground pepper.

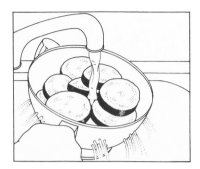

3 Drain the aubergine slices, rinse thoroughly under cold running water and pat dry with absorbent kitchen paper or a clean tea towel.

4 Heat a little olive oil in a frying pan and fry the aubergine slices, a few at a time, until golden brown on both sides. Drain on absorbent kitchen paper. Add more oil as required.

5 Layer the aubergine slices, tomato sauce, Mozzarella cheese and half the Parmesan cheese in a greased shallow oven-proof dish, finishing with a layer of aubergine. Scatter over the remaining Parmesan cheese and drizzle over some olive oil.

6 Bake in the oven at 180°C (350°F) mark 4 for 50–60 minutes until the cheese is golden and the sides bubbling. Garnish with a sprig of basil.

BAKED FENNEL

1.30	f	112 cals

700 g (1½ lb) Florence fennel

salt and freshly ground pepper

75 g (3 oz) butter

finely grated zest of 1 large
   thin-skinned lemon and 30 ml
   (2 tbsp) fresh lemon juice

1 Trim the base and top stems of
the fennel, reserving some of
the feathery green tops. Quarter
each head lengthwise. Blanch in
boiling salted water for 5 minutes.

2 Melt the butter in a shallow
flameproof casserole. Remove
from the heat, and then add the
lemon zest together with the
lemon juice. Season.

3 Arrange fennel in the casserole
in a single layer and turn in the
butter. Cover tightly with lid or
kitchen foil and bake in the oven at
150°C (300°F) mark 2 for about 1¼
hours. Garnish with snipped
fennel tops. Serve hot.

FENNEL
Prized for its unusual aniseed
flavour, fennel is called Florence
fennel after the Italian city of
that name – the Italians are very
fond of this vegetable, which
grows prolifically all over the
Mediterranean. It is the bulb of
the vegetable which is used in
this recipe, although the leaves
of the herb fennel and its seeds
are also used in cooking,
particularly with fish.

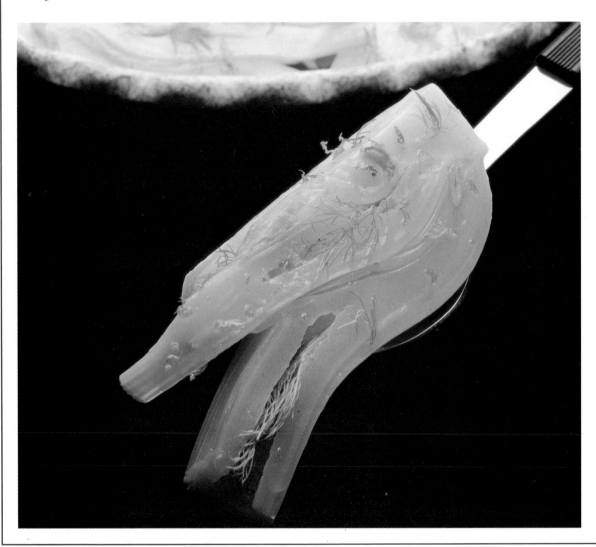

CREAMED BROCCOLI BAKE

1.30	f	220 cals

700 g (1½ lb) broccoli

450 ml (¾ pint) milk

salt and freshly ground pepper

50 g (2 oz) butter or margarine

60 ml (4 tbsp) plain flour

1.25 ml (¼ tsp) grated nutmeg

2 eggs, separated

25 g (1 oz) fresh white breadcrumbs

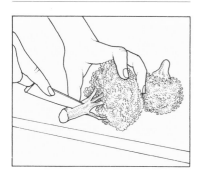

6 Scatter the breadcrumbs over the top, and bake in the oven at 170°C (325°F) mark 3 for about 50 minutes or until the topping has just set. Serve immediately.

5 Whisk the egg whites until stiff, and fold into the sauce. Spoon into a well greased 1.4-litre (2½-pint) shallow ovenproof dish.

1 Trim and discard any thick broccoli stems; cut up the florets into small pieces, then wash and drain well.

2 Place the broccoli in a medium saucepan with the milk and seasoning and bring to the boil. Cover the pan tightly and simmer gently for 10–15 minutes.

3 Strain off the milk and reserve; finely chop the cooked broccoli. Rinse out and dry the saucepan, then melt the butter and stir in the flour. Cook for 1–2 minutes. Gradually stir in the reserved milk (there should be about 300 ml [½ pint]), season well and bring to the boil, bubble for 2 minutes, stirring.

4 Remove from the heat, beat in the chopped broccoli, nutmeg and egg yolks, and adjust seasoning according to taste.

CHINESE STIR-FRY

| 0.20 | £ | 175 cals |

450 g (1 lb) broccoli

350 g (12 oz) carrots

4 large courgettes

salt

30 ml (2 tbsp) sesame seed oil

1 large onion, skinned and finely
   chopped

3 garlic cloves, skinned and
   crushed

2.5-cm (1-inch) piece of fresh root
   ginger, peeled and crushed

225 g (8 oz) beansprouts

45 ml (3 tbsp) soy sauce

30 ml (2 tbsp) clear honey

15 ml (1 tbsp) red wine vinegar

10 ml (2 tsp) tomato purée

30 ml (2 tbsp) vegetable oil

freshly ground pepper

1 Cut the broccoli into bite-sized florets, discarding the thick stalks. Then peel the carrots and cut them into thin matchsticks. Blanch the broccoli and carrots together in boiling salted water for 2 minutes only. Remove with a slotted spoon and set aside.

2 Wash and trim the courgettes, and cut into thin slices. Add to the pan, bring the water back to the boil and blanch for 1 minute only. Drain, reserving 60 ml (4 tbsp) of the water, and set aside.

3 Heat the sesame seed oil in a wok or large, deep frying pan. Add the onion, garlic and ginger and fry gently until soft and lightly coloured. Add the beansprouts and stir-fry for 2 minutes only. Remove with a slotted spoon and set aside until ready to serve.

4 In a separate jug or bowl, mix the reserved blanching water with the soy sauce, honey, vinegar and tomato purée.

5 Heat the vegetable oil in the wok, add the blanched vegetables and stir-fry for 2 minutes or until heated through.

6 Pour in the soy sauce mixture and add the beansprouts, then stir-fry for 1–2 minutes until very hot. Add salt and pepper to taste, turn into a warmed serving dish and serve immediately.

COURGETTES WITH MUSHROOMS

| 0.50 | £ | 166 cals |

1.1 kg (2½ lb) courgettes

50 g (2 oz) butter

salt and freshly ground pepper

225 g (8 oz) button mushrooms, wiped

142 ml (5 fl oz) soured cream

fresh basil sprig, to garnish

1 Wash the courgettes under cold running water. Then wipe and slice them into 0.5-cm (¼-inch) pieces, discarding the ends.

2 Melt the butter in a medium roasting tin, add the courgettes and turn over in the butter; season well with salt and pepper.

3 Bake the courgette slices in the oven at 200°C (400°F) mark 6 for about 20 minutes.

4 Meanwhile, trim and slice the mushrooms. Stir into the courgettes and return to the oven for a further 10–15 minutes.

5 Stir the soured cream and then mix through the vegetables; bubble up on top of the stove. To serve, adjust seasoning and spoon the vegetables into a serving dish. Garnish with the basil.

VARIATION

Single cream, with a squeeze of **lemon juice**, can be substituted for the **soured cream**. Stir into the vegetables and heat gently but do not boil.

French beans or **florets of young broccoli** or **cauliflower** can be used instead of the courgettes.

Make sure that the cream does not boil or it might curdle.

CAULIFLOWER AND COURGETTE TARTLETS

| 1.00* | 🍽 | 🍽 | £ | 251 cals |

* plus 2–3 hours chilling time and 2
hours cooling time

75 ml (5 tbsp) dry white wine

30 ml (2 tbsp) vegetable oil

5 ml (1 tsp) chopped fresh tarragon
or 1.25 ml ($\frac{1}{4}$ tsp) dried

1 garlic clove, skinned and crushed

salt and freshly ground pepper

225-g (8 oz) cauliflower, trimmed
and cut into small florets

175 g (6 oz) baby courgettes

100 g (4 oz) plain flour

50 g (2 oz) plain wholemeal flour

75 g (3 oz) butter

15–30 ml (1–2 tbsp) water

1 To make the dressing, in a medium bowl, whisk together the wine, oil, tarragon, crushed garlic and seasoning.

2 Blanch the cauliflower florets in boiling salted water for 1 minute only. Drain well, then, while still hot, stir into the dressing.

3 Slice the courgettes into thin rings and add to the bowl, stirring gently to mix. Leave to cool, then cover with cling film and refrigerate for several hours or overnight.

4 Make pastry. Mix flours together with pinch of salt. Rub in the butter until the mixture resembles fine breadcrumbs; bind to a dough with water.

5 Knead the pastry lightly until just smooth, then roll out and use to line six 7.5-cm (3-inch) individual flan tins.

6 Bake blind (see page 153) in the oven at 200°C (400°F) mark 6 for about 15 minutes or until just set and tinged with colour. Remove the paper and baking beans and return to the oven for a further 8–10 minutes or until well browned.

7 Cool slightly, ease cases out of tins and leave for 2 hours until completely cool. Store in an airtight container until required.

8 Just before serving, place the pastry cases on individual plates and spoon in the cauliflower and courgette salad.

GREEN BEANS WITH COCONUT

0.15* £ 165 cals

* 8 minutes if using mange-tout

700 g (1½ lb) fresh or frozen green
    beans or mange tout

salt

1 onion, skinned

50 g (2 oz) butter or margarine

50 g (2 oz) desiccated coconut

freshly ground pepper

45 ml (3 tbsp) chopped fresh
    parsley

1 Cook the beans in boiling salted water for 10 minutes, or 3 minutes for fresh mange tout (for frozen vegetables, follow packet instructions), until cooked but firm to the bite.

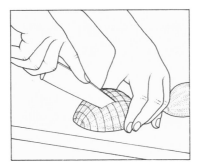

2 Meanwhile, finely chop the onion. Heat the butter in a small frying pan, add the onion and cook gently until softened, stirring occasionally.

3 Increase heat, add coconut and fry for 2–3 minutes until golden. Season and mix in parsley. Drain beans and spoon into a serving dish and sprinkle over coconut mixture.

COCONUT

Desiccated coconut is used in this recipe, but if you can buy a fresh coconut, then so much the better. Simply pierce a hole in its shell and drain off the milk, then crack the shell open with a hammer and dig out the flesh. Grate the flesh finely on a conical or box grater – you will find it far sweeter and juicier than desiccated coconut. Shredded coconut, which comes in large flakes, can also be used if your prefer: it is available at health food shops.

Children's Birthday Party for 10 six year-olds

BIRTHDAY PARCEL CAKE

| 1.00* | 🎂 🎂 £ ✳* | 368 cals |

* plus overnight setting; freeze basic cake before adding decoration

Serves 10

175 g (6 oz) plain flour
7.5 ml (1½ tsp) baking powder
175 g (6 oz) soft tub margarine
175 g (6 oz) caster sugar
3 eggs
5 ml (1 tsp) vanilla flavouring
100 g (4 oz) butter, softened
225 g (8 oz) icing sugar, sifted
10 ml (2 tsp) lemon juice
225 g (8 oz) marzipan
1 egg white, lightly beaten
600 g (1¼ lb) white fondant icing
food colouring

1 Sift the flour and baking powder into a bowl. Add margarine, caster sugar, eggs and vanilla flavouring, then beat for 1–2 minutes until light and fluffy. Divide evenly between two greased and lined 18-cm (7½-inch) square cake tins.

2 Bake in the oven at 190°C (375°F) gas 5 for 20 minutes or until the centres of the cakes spring back when lightly pressed with the fingertips. Leave to cool in the tins for 2 minutes, then turn both cakes out on to a wire rack and cool.

3 Make the buttercream. Beat the butter in a bowl until light and fluffy, then gradually beat in the icing sugar until well blended. Stir in the lemon juice.

4 Sandwich the cakes together with all but 30 ml (2 tbsp) of the buttercream. Put the cake on a cake board and spread the reserved buttercream smoothly over the top and sides. Set aside.

5 For the decoration, knead the marzipan until pliable, then knead in a few drops of food colouring until evenly coloured.

6 Roll out on a surface lightly sprinkled with icing sugar to the following shapes: two strips measuring 30 × 2.5 cm (12 × 1 inch), three strips measuring 15 × 2.5 cm (6 × 1 inch); one strip measuring 7.5 × 2.5 cm (3 × 1 inch); one strip measuring 5 × 2.5 cm (2 × 1 inch). Set aside.

7 Knead the fondant icing until smooth and pliable. Put a small amount aside for the gift tag and thread, then roll out the remainder to a 30-cm (12-inch) square. Place over cake and mitre the corners like a parcel.

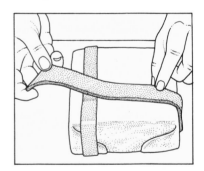

8 Brush one side of the 30-cm (12-inch)-long strips with a little of the beaten egg white, then place them this side down on top of the cake to look like ribbon on a parcel.

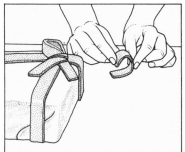

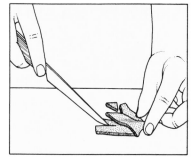

FINISHING THE DECORATION

If you are feeling artistic, finish off the cake by drawing a design on the fondant to make it look like wrapping paper. The simplest way to do this is to use edible food colouring pens. Available from specialist kitchen shops, they look just like felt tips. Don't forget to finish off tag.

9 Loop the three 15-cm (6-inch) strips to look like a bow and fix on top of cake with egg white. Use 7.5-cm (3-inch) strip to form the centre of the bow.

10 Cut 5-cm (2-inch) strip in a V-shape to form end of ribbon. Fix into place with egg white. Use reserved fondant to make tag and thread, then fix on cake. Leave overnight.

CHEESE STICKS

0.30	£	✳	84 cals

Makes about 100 sticks

100 g (4 oz) plain flour
pinch of salt
50 g (2 oz) butter or margarine
50 g (2 oz) mature Cheddar cheese
1 egg, beaten
Parmesan cheese, grated

1 Mix the flour and salt in a bowl. Rub in fat until mixture resembles fine breadcrumbs.

2 Grate in the cheddar, using a Mouli or other fine grater. Bind together with a little beaten egg and knead lightly.

3 Roll out on a floured surface to an oblong 25.5 × 15 cm (10 × 6 inch). Brush with beaten egg; sprinkle liberally with Parmesan. Press cheese lightly into egg.

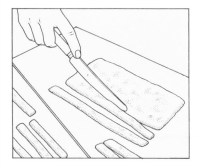

4 Cut into sticks 6 cm × 0.5 cm (2½ × ¼ inch) and place on ungreased baking sheets. Bake in the oven at 200°C (400°F) mark 6 for 10 minutes until golden. Cool.

PICKLE PIZZA SQUARES

| 0.50 | £ | ✳ | 304 cals |

Makes 10 slices

75 g (3 oz) margarine
275 g (10 oz) plain wholemeal flour
salt and freshly ground pepper
7.5 ml (1½ tsp) baking powder
45 ml (3 tbsp) tomato relish
30 ml (2 tbsp) water
1 onion, skinned
175 g (6 oz) luncheon meat or ham
100 g (4 oz) Cheddar cheese, grated
1 egg, size 2, beaten
2 rashers of streaky bacon

1 In a large bowl rub margarine into the flour, salt and baking powder. Stir in tomato relish and the water.

2 Bind to a smooth manageable dough. Roll out into a 33 × 23 cm (13 × 9 inch) rectangle. Trim the edges with a knife.

3 Finely chop the onion and meat. Combine with the cheese and stir in the egg. Season. Cut bacon in thin strips.

4 Spread the mixture evenly over the surface to cover the dough. Garnish with the bacon strips, arranged in a pattern.

5 Bake in the oven at 190°C (375°F) mark 5 for about 30 minutes until the cheese bubbles up and is golden and the dough is cooked. Serve hot cut into squares.

CUCUMBER CROCODILE WITH TOMATO DIP AND DUNKS

| 0.45 | ⛶ ⛶ | 348 cals |

Serves 10

450 g (1 lb) chipolata sausages
225 g (8 oz) Cheddar cheese
1 large, slightly curved cucumber
150 ml (¼ pint) mayonnaise
30 ml (2 tbsp) tomato ketchup
salt and freshly ground pepper
celery, carrots and cucumber
   sticks, to serve

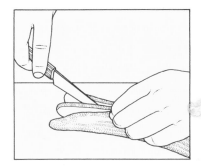

1 Twist each chipolata into two and snip apart. Cook in the oven at 190°C (375°F) mark 5 for about 20 minutes until golden. Place on cocktail sticks. Cut the cheese into 1-cm (½-inch) cubes. Place on cocktail sticks. Mix together the mayonnaise, tomato ketchup and seasoning. Spoon into a small bowl, cover and chill well.

2 To make the crocodile, cut out a 7.5 cm (3 inch) wedge of cucumber to form the mouth. Then cut out the teeth. Cut out a small hole for the eyes and press in a small piece of tomato. Arrange sausage and cheese cubes in crocodile.

3 Serve the dip with the crocodile and the sausages and cheese sticks of celery, crisps, carrot, and cheese sticks (left).

HEDGEHOGS, LADYBIRDS AND TORTOISES

1.00 🥄 🥄 £ ✳* 212 cals

* freeze buns only

Makes 15

50 g (2 oz) butter

50 g (2 oz) caster sugar

1 egg beaten

50 g (2 oz) self-raising flour

15 ml (1 tbsp) milk

For the hedgehogs:

chocolate butter icing, chocolate buttons, silver or gold balls, dolly mixture jellies

For the ladybirds:

75 g (3 oz) marzipan, red edible food colouring, stiff white glacé icing, polka dots

For the tortoises:

175 g (6 oz) marzipan, apricot jam, brown and green edible food colouring, silver balls

1 Cream the butter and sugar together thoroughly then gradually beat in the egg. Lastly fold in the flour and milk.

2 Divide the mixture between fifteen well-greased patty tins with rounded bases. Bake in the oven at 180°C (350°F) mark 4 for about 15 minutes, then leave to cool on wire racks.

3 Make the hedgehogs. Cover five of the cold buns with chocolate butter icing, shaping to form a snout. Decorate with halved chocolate buttons, silver or gold balls for eyes and dolly mixture jellies for snout.

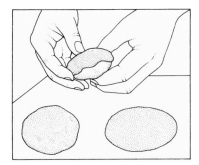

4 Make the ladybirds. Colour the marzipan a deep pink with red colouring, roll out thinly and use to cover a further five buns. Using white glacé icing, pipe lines and spots on to the backs of the ladybirds and use chocolate polka dots for eyes.

5 Make the tortoises. Colour two-thirds of the marzipan a deep green with green colouring, and the remaining third a deep brown with brown colouring. Cover the remaining five buns with a layer of the green marzipan.

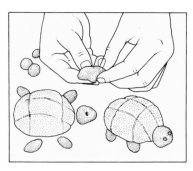

6 With a skewer mark on the 'shell' markings. Use the brown marzipan to form heads, legs and tails and attach to the tortoise body with a little jam. Make eyes with silver balls.

Desserts

Go to town on the dessert course – everyone will appreciate it! A spectacular finale to a dinner party is never a wasted effort, and the compliments from your guests will make you feel that all your efforts have been worthwhile.

To complement your dessert, serve it with a white dessert wine such as a good sweet Sauternes, the perfect end to a perfect meal.

ALMOND AND COFFEE MERINGUE CAKE

| 1.45* | 🔲 🔲 £ £ ✳* | 485 cals |

* plus 1 hour cooling and chilling; freeze before decorating

3 egg whites
175 g (6 oz) granulated sugar
50 g (2 oz) ground almonds
50 g (2 oz) whole unblanched almonds
50 g (2 oz) caster sugar
300 ml (10 fl oz) double or whipping cream
45 ml (3 tbsp) coffee-flavoured liqueur

1 Draw two 20.5-cm (8-inch) circles on non-stick paper and place them face down on baking sheets so the pencil marks don't come in contact with the food.

2 To make the meringue, whisk the egg whites until stiff, then gradually whisk in the granulated sugar, keeping the mixture stiff; fold in the ground almonds.

3 Spread out the meringue into the circles marked on the paper. Bake in the oven at 150°C (300°F) mark 2 for about 1 hour until well browned and crisp.

4 Cool slightly, then ease off the non-stick paper and place the meringue rounds on a wire rack to cool completely.

5 Meanwhile, make the praline. Place the whole almonds and caster sugar in a small saucepan. Heat gently, turning the nuts over occasionally, until the sugar melts and caramelises.

6 When the sugar is well browned, pour the almond mixture out on to an oiled, edged baking sheet and leave to cool and harden.

7 Ease the cold praline off the baking sheet and remove any surface oil with absorbent kitchen paper.

8 Grind half the praline using a rolling pin or a nut mouli, or crush in a pestle and mortar. In a separate bowl, whip the cream until it holds its shape, whisk in the coffee liqueur and fold in the crushed praline.

9 Sandwich the meringue rounds with the cream and decorate with reserved broken praline. Refrigerate for at least 1 hour and not more than 3 hours before serving.

Menu Suggestion
Serve with Mousseline of Sole with Prawns (page 12) and Boned Stuffed Poussins (page 66).

MERINGUE CAKES
There are three basic types of meringue. Meringue suisse, the easiest to make has a crisp texture and is used for shells and nests. Meringue cuite is a more stable mixture, ideal for piping fancy baskets and cases. It is more brittle and powdery than meringue suisse. American meringue is used for pavlovas, layered tortes and party cakes.

The unique texture of this meringue – crisp outside and marshmallowy within – is due to the addition of a little vinegar and cornflour.

For best results, use eggs that are 2–3 days old. If possible, keep the separated whites – which must be quite free of any yolk – in a covered container in the refrigerator for up to 24 hours before use.

CRÊPES ANNETTE

| 1.00 | 🍴 🍴 £ £ ✳* | 91 cals |

* unfilled crêpes can be frozen

250 g (9 oz) plain flour

5 ml (1 tsp) baking powder

2.5 ml ($\frac{1}{2}$ tsp) bicarbonate of soda

pinch of salt

165 ml (9 tbsp) kirsch

568 ml (1 pint) milk

25 g (1 oz) butter, melted

2 eggs, beaten

vegetable oil, for frying

425-g (15-oz) can black cherries

175 g (6 oz) full fat soft cheese

50 g (2 oz) caster sugar

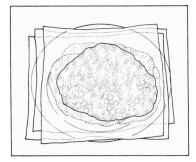

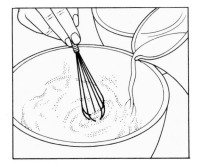

1 Make the crêpes. Sift flour with baking powder, soda and salt. Add 105 ml (6 tbsp) kirsch and next three ingredients and beat until smooth.

2 Heat a little oil in a heavy-based frying pan. Pour in 30 ml (2 tbsp) batter. Swirl around pan; cook until golden under-neath. Flip over and cook on the other side.

3 Turn the crêpe out on to a plate lined with a sheet of greaseproof paper and keep warm in a low oven. Repeat with the remaining batter to make twelve crêpes in all, stacking them in a pile with greaseproof paper in between each one. Keep warm.

4 Drain the cherries; reserve the juice and a few cherries. Pit the cherries, if necessary. Beat the cheese and sugar together until soft and fluffy. Chop the remaining cherries roughly and fold them into the cheese.

5 Spread a little filling on each crêpe and fold into triangles; or put the filling in the centre and roll the crêpes up. Keep warm.

6 Heat reserved cherries and syrup in a pan. Gently warm the remaining kirsch. Drizzle the cherries and syrup over the crêpes, then add the kirsch and set alight.

Menu Suggestion
Serve with Avocado with Parma Ham (page 10) and Monkfish and Mussel Brochettes (page 82).

GOOSEBERRY CHARLOTTE

0.50* 🍶 🍶 £ £ ✳* 457 cals

* plus 45 minutes cooling time and 2
  hours setting time; freeze at the end
  of step 7

450 g (1 lb) gooseberries, topped
  and tailed

90 ml (6 tbsp) water

75 g (3 oz) caster sugar

10 ml (2 tsp) gelatine

2 egg yolks

300 ml (½ pint) milk

300 ml (10 fl oz) double cream

20 langue de chat biscuits,
  trimmed to size

angelica, to decorate

1 Wash the gooseberries and
drain well. Place in a small
saucepan with 60 ml (4 tbsp)
water. Cover the pan and simmer
for about 10 minutes until the fruit
softens to a pulpy consistency.

2 Purée in a blender or food
processor, then sieve to
remove the pips. Stir in 50 g (2 oz)
of the sugar. Place 30 ml (2 tbsp)
water into a bowl and sprinkle in
the gelatine. Allow the gelatine to
soak until it has become spongy.

3 Meanwhile, make the custard.
Beat the egg yolks with
remaining sugar until light in
colour. In a small saucepan, warm
the milk, and pour over the eggs
and sugar, stirring until blended.

4 Return to the pan and cook
over a low heat, stirring all the
time, until the custard thickens
sufficiently to lightly coat the back
of the spoon – do not boil.

5 Take off the heat and immediately add the soaked gelatine;
stir until dissolved. Pour the
custard out into a large bowl and
mix in the gooseberry purée, leave
for 45 minutes to cool.

6 Lightly whip the cream and
when the gooseberry mixture
is cold, but not set, stir in half the
cream until evenly blended.

7 Oil and base line a 15-cm
(6-inch) soufflé type non-metal
straight sided dish and pour in the
gooseberry mixture. Refrigerate
for 1–2 hours to set. When firm,
turn out on to a flat serving plate.

8 Spread a thin covering of the
remaining cream around the
edge of the charlotte.

9 Spoon the rest of the cream
into a piping bag fitted with a
1-cm (½-inch) large star nozzle,
and pipe the cream around the top
edge. Decorate with angelica. Just
before serving arrange the biscuits
carefully around the outside.

Menu Suggestion
Serve with Mousseline of Sole
with Prawns (page 12) and Duckling with Brandy and Green
Peppercorn Sauce (page 68).

GOOSEBERRIES
There are many varieties, round
or long, hairy or smooth, cooking
or dessert. Their pale green
colour and unique flavour make
them unbeatable for fruit fools.
  Cooking gooseberries, used in
pies and puddings and for jam,
etc, are usually green, very sour,
with firm flesh and a fairly large
number of seeds. Dessert gooseberries can be green, yellow-
white or a russet colour, often
with a hairy skin, and they
usually have soft, pulpy, sweet
flesh and large seeds.

MANGO ICE CREAM

| 0.30* | 🗂 £ £ ❄ | 354 cals |

* plus 3–4 hours freezing time and 30 minutes to soften

300 ml (½ pint) milk

90 ml (6 tbsp) caster sugar

2 eggs, beaten

2 medium mangoes

300 ml (10 fl oz) double cream

1 Heat milk and sugar in a saucepan. Pour on to eggs and stir well. Return mixture to pan and cook gently, stirring all the time, until thickened. Cover with dampened greaseproof paper; cool.

2 Peel the mangoes and cut the flesh from the stone. Mash or purée flesh in a blender; add to custard.

3 Lightly whip the cream and fold into custard. Pour into a shallow container and freeze for 1 hour until firm around the edge.

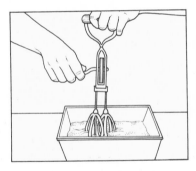

4 Remove from the freezer and beat well to break down ice crystals. Freeze for 2–3 hours until firm. To serve, remove from the freezer and refrigerate for 30 minutes.

Menu Suggestion
Serve with Avocado with Parma Ham (page 10) and Beef in Brandy and Mustard (page 36).

INDIVIDUAL CHOCOLATE MOUSSES

| 0.20* | £ £ ✳* | 531 cals |

* plus 2–3 hours chilling

350 g (12 oz) plain chocolate

6 eggs, separated

30 ml (2 tbsp) rum or brandy

150 ml (5 fl oz) double cream

chocolate curls, to decorate

1 Break the chocolate into a bowl. Place the bowl over a pan of simmering water and heat until melted, stirring occasionally.

2 Remove from heat and beat in egg yolks and rum. Add stiffly whisked egg whites. Spoon into six ramekin dishes and chill for 2–3 hours until set. Whip the cream until stiff. Decorate the mousses with piped cream and chocolate curls.

Menu Suggestion
Serve with Avocado and Kiwi Fruit Vinaigrette (page 125) and Chicken with Tarragon Mayonnaise (page 58).

RASPBERRY AND APPLE TORTE

1.20* 📦 📦 ✳ 467 cals

* plus 2–3 hours chilling

450 g (1 lb) eating apples, peeled and cored

150 g (5 oz) butter or block margarine

450 g (1 lb) fresh raspberries, washed and hulled

65 g (2½ oz) demerara sugar

5 ml (1 tsp) lemon juice

225 g (8 oz) plain flour

10 ml (2 tsp) ground cinnamon

25 g (1 oz) icing sugar

1 egg, separated

45 ml (3 tbsp) water

few fresh raspberries (optional)

1 Quarter and roughly chop the apples. Melt 25 g (1 oz) butter in a medium saucepan, then add the apples, raspberries and 50 g (2 oz) demerara sugar.

2 Heat gently until the sugar dissolves. Increase the heat and cook, stirring, for about 10 minutes or until the apples are soft.

3 Turn the mixture into a bowl, stir in the lemon juice and cool for 30 minutes. Meanwhile, sift the flour and cinnamon into a mixing bowl.

4 Cut and rub in the remaining butter until the mixture resembles fine breadcrumbs. Stir in the icing sugar. Mix the egg yolk with the water and stir into pastry mixture; knead lightly.

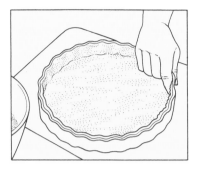

5 Roll out two-thirds of the pastry and use to line a 23-cm (9-inch) fluted flan dish. Spoon in raspberry and apple mixture.

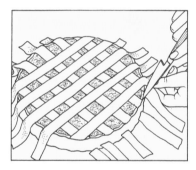

6 Roll out remaining third of pastry and cut into 1-cm (½-inch) wide strips long enough to make a lattice. Trim to fit.

7 Place on a baking sheet and bake in the oven at 200°C (400°F) mark 6 for about 15 minutes or until the pastry is set but not browned.

8 Lightly whisk the egg white, brush over lattice; sprinkle with remaining demerara sugar.

9 Return to the oven for a further 15–20 minutes or until browned. Chill for 2–3 hours before serving. Decorate with a few fresh raspberries, if wished.

Menu Suggestion

Serve with Feta Cheese Soufflé (page 10) and Guard of Honour (page 40).

ALMOND PEACH BRÛLÉES

0.20* £ £	290 cals

* plus at least 9 hours chilling

6 large, ripe peaches

30 ml (2 tbsp) lemon juice

150 ml (5 fl oz) double cream

30 ml (2 tbsp) icing sugar

30 ml (2 tbsp) almond-flavoured liqueur or few drops of almond flavouring

142 ml (5 fl oz) soured cream

90–120 ml (6–8 tbsp) demerara sugar

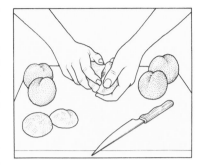

1 Peel the peaches by dipping them in boiling water for about 30 seconds. Plunge them immediately into cold water; peel off the skins. Cut the peaches in half. Twist to separate; remove stones. Thinly slice flesh, toss in lemon juice and set aside.

2 Whip the double cream with the icing sugar until it just holds its shape. Gradually whisk in the liqueur or almond flavouring. Fold in the soured cream and peach slices.

3 Divide this mixture between six 150-ml ($\frac{1}{4}$-pint) ramekin dishes. Cover and chill overnight. Sprinkle enough demerara sugar on top to form a covering.

4 Place under a hot grill for 3–4 minutes until the sugar has caramelised. Chill for about 1 hour.

Menu Suggestion
Serve with Chestnut and Orange Soup (page 9) and Beef Wellington (page 34).

MELON AND GINGER SORBET

| 0.30* £ ✳ | 80 cals |

* plus 6 hours freezing and 30 minutes
  softening

75 g (3 oz) sugar

1 medium honeydew melon

45 ml (3 tbsp) lemon juice

1 piece preserved stem ginger,
  finely chopped

few drops green food colouring
  (optional)

2 egg whites

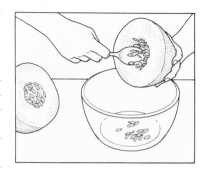

1 Dissolve the sugar slowly in
300 ml (½ pint) water. Bring to
the boil, bubble for 2 minutes,
then transfer to a bowl and leave
the sugar syrup to cool.

2 Halve the melon, remove the
seeds and scoop out the flesh.
Purée the flesh in a blender or a
food processor until smooth. Stir
into the cool syrup with the lemon
juice. Then add the chopped stem
ginger and a few drops of green
food colouring, if wished.

3 Freeze the sorbet in a shallow
container for about 3 hours
until mushy in texture. Whisk the
egg whites until stiff and fold into
the sorbet mixture. Return to the
freezer for a further 3 hours until
the sorbet is firm.

4 To serve, remove from the
freezer and place in the refrigerator for about 30 minutes to
soften slightly. Serve in individual
glasses, with fan wafers if liked.

Menu Suggestion
Serve with Iced Tzaziki Soup
(page 86) and Malaysian-style
Prawns (page 84).

FRESH PEAR SHORTCAKE

1.45 £ ✳ 444 cals
150 g (5 oz) self-raising flour
25 g (1 oz) ground rice
grated rind of 1 lemon
50 g (2 oz) soft dark brown sugar
150 g (5 oz) butter
3 ripe large, even-sized pears, about 450 g (1 lb) in weight
125 g (4 oz) full fat soft cheese
1 egg
few drops almond flavouring

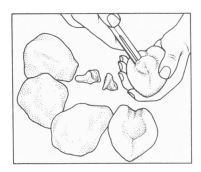

1 Lightly grease a 20.5-cm (8-inch) loose-based fluted flan tin and set aside. In a mixing bowl, stir together the self-raising flour, ground rice and the grated lemon rind and mix them well.

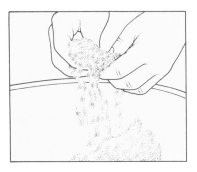

2 Sieve the soft dark brown sugar into the bowl. Rub in the butter and continue lightly kneading the mixture until it forms a dough.

3 Press the dough into the prepared tin with floured fingertips. Mark into six portions and prick well with a fork.

4 Bake in the oven at 190°C (375°F) mark 5 for 30–35 minutes until light brown and cooked through. Leave in the tin to cool slightly.

5 Using a sharp knife, peel and halve the pears. Then scoop out the cores using a teaspoon or corer. Discard the cores.

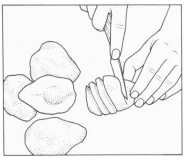

6 Slice each pear half crosswise, into pieces 3-mm ($\frac{1}{8}$-inch) thick, keeping the slices together. Then place a sliced pear half on each portion of shortcake, fanning out the slices a little.

7 Beat together the soft cheese, egg and almond flavouring until smooth, then spoon over the pears, completely covering both fruit and shortcake.

8 Bake in the oven at 180°C (350°F) mark 4 for 40 minutes until golden. Ease out of the tin and serve warm or cold.

Menu Suggestion
Serve with Stuffed Globe Artichokes (page 14) and Baked Trout with Lemon (page 77).

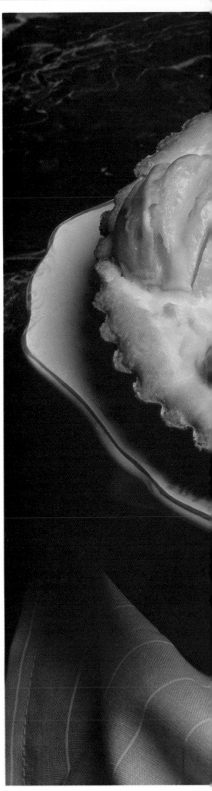

PINEAPPLE CHEESECAKE

2.15*	£ £ ✳*	720 cals

* plus 2 hours standing time in oven
and 2 hours cooling time; freeze
without topping

| 50 g (2 oz) digestive biscuits |
| 15 g ($\frac{1}{2}$ oz) butter |
| 4 eggs, size 2, separated |
| 225 g (8 oz) caster sugar |
| 450 g (1 lb) full fat soft cheese |
| 40 g (1$\frac{1}{2}$ oz) plain flour, sifted |
| 30 ml (2 tbsp) lemon juice |
| 284 ml (10 fl oz) soured cream |
| 432-g (14$\frac{1}{2}$-oz) can pineapple slices |
| 20 ml (4 tsp) arrowroot |
| 300 ml (10 fl oz) double cream |
| 90 g (3$\frac{1}{2}$ oz) walnut halves |

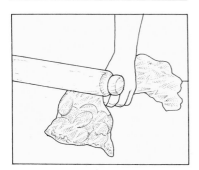

1 Put the biscuits in a strong
polythene bag and crush them
with a rolling pin. Lightly grease
a 19-cm (7$\frac{1}{2}$-inch) round loose-
bottomed cake tin and set aside.

2 Melt the butter and stir in the
biscuit crumbs. Press this mixture over the base of the tin. Chill
for 30 minutes to set.

3 Whisk the egg yolks with the
sugar until thick and creamy.
In a separate bowl, beat the cheese
lightly. Add the whisked mixture
to the cheese and mix until
smooth. Stir in the flour, lemon
juice and soured cream.

4 Whisk the egg whites until stiff
and fold into the cheese and
lemon mixture. Pour into the cake
tin and level the surface.

5 Bake in the oven at 130°C
(250°F) mark $\frac{1}{2}$ for 1$\frac{1}{2}$ hours.
Turn off the heat and leave in the
oven for 2 hours without opening
the door. Remove from the oven
and leave for 2 hours to cool in the
tin. When cool, carefully remove
cheesecake from the tin.

6 Drain the pineapple, reserving
150 ml ($\frac{1}{4}$ pint) syrup, and
arrange over the top of the cheesecake. Blend the arrowroot with a
little of the syrup. Bring the
remaining syrup to the boil.

7 Add the arrowroot and, stirring
all the time, cook for a few
minutes until thickened. Leave to
cool slightly, then spoon the syrup
over the pineapple on top of the
cheesecake.

8 Finely chop the walnuts, reserving twelve halves. Whip
the cream until stiff and spread a
little over the sides of the cheesecake, reserving a little for decoration.

9 Press the chopped walnuts
around the sides. Pipe the remaining cream on top and decorate with walnut halves.

Menu Suggestion
Serve with Italian Squid Salad
(pages 16–17) and Pork Loin with
Cider (page 43).

—— ALTERNATIVE TOPPINGS ——

142 ml (5 fl oz) soured cream
and **25 g (1 oz) toasted flaked
almonds** sprinkled on top.

**225 g (8 oz) fresh strawberries,
hulled,** and **150 ml (5 fl oz)
whipping cream,** piped in
rosettes.

PETITS FOURS

RUM TRUFFLES

| 0.25* | £ £ | 103 cals |

* plus 30 minutes setting time and
  30 minutes chilling

Makes 12–14

125 g (4 oz) plain chocolate

12.5 ml (2½ tsp) rum

1 egg yolk

25 g (1 oz) cake crumbs

25 g (1 oz) icing sugar

chocolate vermicelli

1 To make the truffle mixture, melt the chocolate in a small bowl over a pan of hot water and add the rum. It is important that the mixture doesn't get too hot. When melted, stir in the egg yolk and cook, stirring all the time, until the truffle mixture begins to thicken very slightly.

2 Remove the bowl from the heat and gently stir in the cake crumbs and icing sugar. Continue stirring until mixture cools a little.

3 Place the prepared truffle mixture in the refrigerator and leave for about 30 minutes until it is almost set.

4 Divide the mixture into twelve pieces. With a little icing sugar on your hands, roll the mixture into balls. Roll each ball in the vermicelli and place in individual paper cases.

5 Store, covered, in the refrigerator. Take out of the refrigerator about 30 minutes before serving.

TURKISH DELIGHT

| 0.45* | ▢ ▢ £ | 74 cals |

* plus 24 hours cooling

Makes about 550 g (1¼ lb)

300 ml (½ pint) water

25 g (1 oz) gelatine

450 g (1 lb) granulated sugar

1.25 ml (¼ tsp) citric acid

few drops of vanilla flavouring

few drops of almond flavouring

few drops of red and green food
  colouring

few drops of red food colouring

50 g (2 oz) icing sugar

25 g (1 oz) cornflour

1 Have ready a 20.5 × 15-cm (8 × 6-inch) tin. Put the water in a heavy-based saucepan. Sprinkle the gelatine over it, add the sugar and citric acid and heat slowly until the sugar has dissolved. Bring to the boil and boil for 20 minutes.

2 Remove from the heat and leave to stand for 10 minutes without stirring. Add the flavourings and a few drops of food colouring and pour the mixture into the dampened tin. Leave in a cool place for 24 hours.

3 Sift the icing sugar and the cornflour together and sprinkle them evenly over a piece of greaseproof paper.

4 Turn the Turkish delight out on to the paper and cut it into 48 squares with a sharp knife. Toss in sugar mixture, then pack in greaseproof paper and store in an airtight tin.

ALMOND STARS

| 0.40 | £ £ ✳ | 110 cals |

Makes about 24

2 egg whites

150 g (5 oz) ground almonds

75 g (3 oz) caster sugar

few drops of almond flavouring

24 pieces of angelica or glacé
  cherries, to decorate

1 Line two baking sheets with greaseproof paper. Whisk the egg whites until stiff and use a tablespoon to fold in the almonds, sugar and almond flavouring.

2 Using a large star vegetable nozzle, pipe the almond-flavoured stars, quite close together, on to the lined baking sheets.

3 Decorate each star with a piece of angelica or a glacé cherry. Bake in the oven at 150°C (300°F) mark 2 for 15–20 minutes until just beginning to colour.

PETITS FOURS
Petits fours are the delicious, rich little sweets and biscuits that are served with coffee after dinner.

Traditional petits fours often include little iced cakes made from a Genoese sponge mixture cut into small shapes – triangles, squares, rounds or shapes cut with small fancy cutters. They are coated with apricot jam and then covered with fondant, marzipan or glacé icing. They may be decorated with nuts, glacé fruits, or crystallised flowers.

Christmas Lunch for 8 People

MENU

AVOCADO AND KIWI FRUIT
VINAIGRETTE

———————— · ————————

FESTIVE TURKEY SURPRISE

———————— · ————————

SPECIAL FRIED SPROUTS

———————— · ————————

ONIONS À LA GRECQUE

———————— · ————————

ICED CHRISTMAS PUDDING

———————— · ————————

MULLED WINE (page 139)

AVOCADO AND KIWI FRUIT VINAIGRETTE

0.15*	£ £	295 cals

* plus 2 hours refrigeration

Serves 8

1 egg

150 ml ($\frac{1}{4}$ pint) olive oil

60 ml (4 tbsp) white wine vinegar

45 ml (3 tbsp) chopped parsley

salt and freshly ground pepper

4 kiwi fruit

3 small ripe avocados

watercress sprigs, to garnish

French bread, to serve

1 Boil the egg for 6 minutes only. Meanwhile, whisk together the oil, vinegar, parsley and seasonings in a medium bowl.

2 Run cold water over the boiled egg to cool. Shell the egg. Scoop out the yolk into the dressing. Chop the egg white finely and add to the dressing, whisking well to ensure it is evenly mixed.

3 Peel the kiwi fruit and slice it into rings, discarding the ends. Stir into the dressing, cover and refrigerate for at least 2 hours.

4 Halve, peel and slice the avocados and arrange on individual serving plates together with the drained kiwi fruit slices.

5 Spoon the dressing over the avocados and kiwi fruit and garnish with watercress sprigs. Serve with crusty French bread.

AVOCADOS

Avocados are available all year round in supermarkets and greengrocers, and different types are sold according to the time of year and country of origin. They are rich in vitamin C and unsaturated fats. The commonest variety of avocado has a smooth, green, shiny skin, but others with rough skins which darken when ripe, are becoming increasingly widely available. Both types have soft, pale green flesh, and are suitable for use in this recipe.

Only use ripe avocados in salads. To test for ripeness, press fruit gently at the pointed end with your fingers – it should give slightly. When buying avocados, if you are not eating them on the day of purchase, it is best to buy them under-ripe rather than just ripe. Wrap them in newspaper and leave them in a warm place to ripen.

FESTIVE TURKEY SURPRISE

| 4.35 | 🍳 🍳 | £ £ | 402 cals |

Serves about 20

3.9 kg (8½ lb) oven-ready turkey

1 onion, skinned and chopped

100 g (4 oz) celery, finely chopped

450 g (1 lb) cooking apples, peeled, cored and roughly chopped

100 g (4 oz) butter

700 g (1½ lb) pork sausagemeat

50 g (2 oz) fresh white breadcrumbs

grated rind and juice of an orange

50 g (2 oz) chopped walnuts

2.5 ml (½ tsp) dried thyme

salt and freshly ground pepper

2 eggs, size 6, beaten

1.4 kg (2½ lb) boneless bacon joint, boiled and skinned

1 Bone the turkey (see page 158), or ask the butcher to do this for you. Sauté the onion, celery and apples together in half the melted butter for 5 minutes; cool.

2 Work into the sausagemeat and breadcrumbs, adding the grated orange rind, walnuts, thyme and seasoning. Bind with the eggs.

3 Lay out the boned bird, flesh side up. Spread the stuffing over the bird, more generously in the thigh positions. Place the cooked bacon joint lengthwise down the centre of the bird.

4 Tuck the neck end in towards the filling, draw the long sides of the bird over the stuffing and sew it neatly together with fine string to completely encase the stuffing. Use overlapping stitches and do not roll too tightly or the bird will burst during cooking. Secure the string loosely for easy removal. Weigh the bird.

5 Place it, breast side up, on foil in a roasting tin. Spread with remaining butter and add the orange juice. Wrap in foil. Weigh.

6 Roast in the oven at 180°C (350°F) mark 4 for 15 minutes per 450 g (1 lb) plus 15 minutes. Unwrap for last 30 minutes, to brown. Serve the turkey hot with bacon rolls and gravy made from the juices, or chill and serve cold. As with traditional roast turkey, this is ideal for eating cold on Boxing Day; quantities have been calculated accordingly.

SPECIAL FRIED SPROUTS

| 0.30 | £ | 140 cals |

Serves 8

900 g (2 lb) Brussels sprouts

salt and freshly ground pepper

75 g (3 oz) butter

450 g (1 lb) button mushrooms, sliced

2.5 ml (½ tsp) grated nutmeg

120 ml (8 tbsp) soured cream

1 Trim the stalks from the sprouts and discard any discoloured or damaged outer leaves. Cut a cross in the base of each sprout with a small, sharp knife.

2 Plunge the sprouts into a large pan of boiling salted water, bring back to the boil and simmer for 15 minutes. Drain thoroughly.

3 Melt the butter in a large, heavy-based pan (a wok or deep frying-pan is ideal). Add the sprouts and mushrooms with the nutmeg, then stir-fry for about 5 minutes until the vegetables are well mixed and heated through.

4 Add salt and pepper to taste, then turn into a warmed serving dish. To serve, stir the soured cream then drizzle over sprouts.

ONIONS À LA GRECQUE

| 1.00 | £ | 172 cals |

Serves 8

900 g (2 lb) small pickling onions
75 ml (5 tbsp) olive oil
15 ml (1 tbsp) clear honey
300 ml ($\frac{1}{2}$ pint) water
150 ml ($\frac{1}{4}$ pint) dry white wine
10 ml (2 tsp) tomato purée
salt and freshly ground pepper
100 g (4 oz) seedless raisins
30 ml (2 tbsp) chopped fresh
   coriander or parsley

1 Peel the onions. Blanch in boiling water for 1 minute only, then drain and rinse under cold running water. Remove the onion skins carefully with your fingers and a small, sharp knife.

2 Put the onions in a large, heavy-based pan with the remaining ingredients except the raisins and chopped coriander.

3 Add salt and pepper to taste. Bring to the boil, then lower the heat, cover and simmer gently for 30 minutes.

4 Add the raisins to the pan and continue cooking, uncovered, for a further 15 minutes or until onions are tender but still whole. Taste and adjust seasoning, then stir in the chopped coriander. Turn into a warmed serving dish and serve hot.

À LA GRECQUE
The French term *à la grecque*, used here to describe a dish of onions, is more commonly used to describe a cold mushroom dish. There are no hard-and-fast rules about the exact ingredients an *à la grecque* dish should contain, but it is usually white wine, tomato purée and raisins, with plenty of chopped parsley.

127

ICED CHRISTMAS PUDDING

0.25* £ £ ✳ 429 cals

* plus 2–3 hours soaking fruit, 30 minutes cooling, 4–5 hours freezing and 20 minutes softening

Serves 8

225 g (8 oz) mixed dried fruit

50 g (2 oz) glacé cherries, halved

75 ml (5 tbsp) brandy

450 ml ($\frac{3}{4}$ pint) milk

3 eggs

140 g ($4\frac{1}{2}$ oz) caster sugar

300 ml (10 fl oz) double cream

150 ml (5 fl oz) single cream

1 Place the mixed dried fruit and glacé cherries in a bowl, spoon over the brandy, cover and leave to soak for 2–3 hours. Bring the milk nearly to boil, beat the eggs with the sugar until well mixed.

2 Pour on the milk, return to the pan and cook over a gentle heat, without boiling, until the custard coats the back of the spoon. Strain and cool for 30 minutes.

3 Whip the creams together, and mix into the custard with the fruit and brandy mixture.

4 Turn into a large bowl and freeze for 2 hours until mushy. Mix well and pack into a 1.7-litre (3-pint) pudding basin base-lined with non-stick paper. Freeze for 2–3 hours until firm.

5 Take out of the freezer approximately 20 minutes before serving. Turn out and decorate with holly. Serve immediately.

USEFUL INFORMATION
AND
BASIC RECIPES

Entertaining at Home

Whether you're planning a buffet party for a hundred, or simply thinking of inviting a few friends round for dinner, this section of the book is designed to help you.

Tips and hints on all kinds of parties are here, from sober morning coffee and afternoon tea to the not–so–sober cocktail party and Champagne wedding reception.

INFORMAL PARTIES

COFFEE MORNINGS AND TEA PARTIES

This type of party can be a purely social occasion for a sizeable number of friends, neighbours and members of the family, such as a christening, or it may arise because there is a committee meeting or some other activity taking place in your home. Whatever the reason, it's a good way of entertaining a large number of people without going to all the expense and effort of a dinner party.

Hand round food on trays lined with paper napkins (enlist a friend to help with the serving), and provide napkins for your guests to use. Serve dainty sandwiches for tea, with crusts cut off and unusual fillings. Different shapes will add interest too, as will small cakes and/or sweet pastries.

In winter, a few hot savoury pastries will be welcome, or some hot buttered scones, crumpets or muffins. Provide both China and Indian tea, with milk and sugar, and also thinly cut slices of lemon for those who prefer it.

For a coffee party, homemade biscuits, pastries and small cakes are sufficient, with perhaps a large cake or gâteau for the table centre-piece. A tray or two of bite-sized open sandwiches will also be welcome, bearing in mind that food shouldn't be too substantial if the party is before lunch – or after dinner in the evening. Always make fresh coffee for this type of party and offer both cream and milk with coffee sugars and crystals.

SANDWICHES AND FILLINGS

If you buy uncut sandwich loaves, you can control the thickness of the slices – and slicing will be considerably simplified – if you use an electric carving knife. Use the following to guide you.

A large loaf, about 800 g (28 oz), gives 20–24 slices.

A small loaf, about 400 g (14 oz), gives 10–12 slices.

A long sandwich loaf, about 1.5 kg (3 lb), gives 50 slices.

About 225 g (8 oz) butter or margarine spreads 10–12 sandwiches.

About 100 g (4 oz) butter or margarine spreads 10–12 bread rolls.

APPROXIMATE COFFEE AND TEA QUANTITIES

	1 Serving	24–26 Servings	Notes
Coffee ground	200 ml ($\frac{1}{3}$ pint)	250–275 g (9–10 oz) coffee 3.6 litres (6 pints) water 1.75 litres (3 pints) milk 450 g (1 lb) sugar	If you make the coffee in advance strain it after infusion. Reheat without boiling.
Tea Indian	200 ml ($\frac{1}{3}$ pint)	50 g (2 oz) tea 4.75 litres (8 pints) water 900 ml ($1\frac{1}{2}$ pints) milk 450 g (1 lb) sugar	It is better to make tea in several pots rather than one outsized one.
China	200 ml ($\frac{1}{3}$ pint)	50 g (2 oz) tea 5.25 litres (9 pints) water 2–3 lemons 450 g (1 lb) sugar	Infuse China tea for 2 or 3 minutes only. Put a thin lemon slice in each cup before pouring. Serve sugar separately.

COCKTAIL PARTIES

A drinks party offers a fairly inexpensive way of entertaining large numbers of people without having to get involved in serious cooking. The term 'cocktail party' is a slight misnomer, however, since usually very few cocktails proper are served. It's perfectly acceptable,

for example, to offer a choice of only two cocktails, with sherry and/or vermouth as a third choice, whisky as a possible fourth, and plenty of fruit juices and soft drinks. If you *are* only serving two cocktails, however, they should be contrasting.

Guests should be well informed about what to expect, in terms of drink, food and time. Cocktail parties should ideally leave people free to go off and enjoy the rest of the evening elsewhere, so the maximum length of time should be about 2 hours. Food should not be so substantial that guests are unable to enjoy their evening meal, nor so paltry that they have to suffer the consequences of drinking on an empty stomach.

Since most people will be drinking and eating standing up, the food must be bite-sized and easy to eat. Canapés are the obvious choice and these and other cocktail nibbles such as nuts, crisps, olives, gherkins, cocktail sausages on sticks, and savoury dips with raw vegetables and bread sticks for dunking can be put out around the room. Try to serve something hot and savoury about halfway through.

CHILDREN'S BIRTHDAY PARTIES

Preparing food for children's parties is a chance to be creative, but there's no need to make *all* the food fancy. Always popular with every age group are crisps, sausages on sticks and other savoury nibbles. Also, sandwiches with plain, everyday fillings go down better than cream cakes and buns.

Don't be surprised either if homemade strawberry tartlets are left and bought biscuits disappear. Children often prefer food that looks familiar. The one exception to this rule is the birthday cake. Never miss it out. Keep the food easy to eat, especially for the very young. All children enjoy fizzy drinks, though sometimes younger children might prefer milk shakes.

Try and keep the number of guests manageable. Organise the programme beforehand. Allow for 1 hour or more of boisterous play before tea and have an entertainment or organised games afterwards. Children over eight can stand more activity, but no party should last longer than 3 hours for small children, or 4 for older ones.

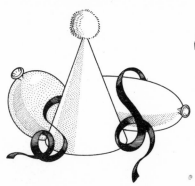

Before the day remember to stock up the first aid box; keep a box of matches at hand – but out of reach of the children – to light the cake candles when the time comes; and have ready masses of small prizes for the winners of the various games. Finally, have a small present and a balloon ready for everyone to take home – it needn't be anything elaborate, but make sure no one is left out.

BARBECUES

Barbecue parties, whether at lunch time or in the evening, are a good idea for entertaining large numbers – people can spread themselves out, so space and eating arrangements are rarely a problem.

Barbecues range from do-it-yourself brick-built affairs to sophisticated (and expensive) equipment. Essential items, however, are equipment such as strong grids, long-handled forks, tongs and slices for turning food, pastry brushes for basting and thick oven gloves to protect the hands. Good-quality charcoal or briquettes, firelighters and matches are other essentials – so too is adequate lighting for evening barbecues.

Self-service is essential: arrange stacks of plates (paper ones will do) on a long table together with glasses, cutlery and napkins and the non-barbecued food. Everyone can then help themselves to these and queue up at the barbecue for hot food. It's not even essential for the host or hostess to do the barbecuing – some guests might like to do it themselves.

If it rains before all the food is cooked, don't ever attempt to barbecue indoors or in the garage because fumes can be dangerous. You will either have to resort to using the grill or cooking under an umbrella. Many of the new barbecues on the market have lids – otherwise you can improvise with a metal dustbin lid.

LARGE BUFFET PARTIES

If you are entertaining a very large number of people and want to provide a full meal, a buffet party is the ideal choice. The maximum number you should try to cater for is 100, however – anything over this is best left to the professionals.

First and foremost, it's virtually impossible to cater for this large a number with the average family's quota of china, cutlery and chairs, so you will have to organise where all this is coming from well in advance. Don't be afraid to ask your friends to help out with plates, serving dishes and so on. A few recruited helpers are essential for the preparation and serving anyway – it would be almost impossible to manage completely on your own for a very large buffet party.

Depending on the formality of the occasion, paper plates and plastic cutlery *can* be considered, although these are not very successful. Good-quality paper napkins and cloths are a better buy, because they come in so many different attractive colours.

Glasses are hardly ever a problem, since your local off-licence will supply these, usually free of charge, if you order the drink from them at the same time. Don't forget to order wines and spirits *well* ahead (especially if your party is around Christmas time), on a 'sale or return' basis if possible.

Decide on the menu really well in advance, because it will take you a long time to finalise quantities (consult our chart for guidance) and the logistics of the whole exercise. The best thing is to have a meeting with your helpers at least a month in advance of the party's date and for you all to make detailed lists of exactly who is doing what, when.

Try to choose food that can be eaten easily without a table: a full set of cutlery should be available, but guests will feel far more comfortable if they are able to eat with a fork alone. For a very large number of people, the majority of food is bound to be cold, but one or two hot dishes will always be welcome.

Offer a good balance of sweet and savoury dishes and concentrate on setting the buffet table beautifully, so that it will be the centre of attraction. Choose dishes that can be frozen ahead of time

(most things store well in the freezer for at least three months) like quiches, flans, pâtés, tarts, pastries, sandwich fillings, cakes and gâteaux. This should leave you ample time nearer the date to deal with the perishable items like salads.

Having the right equipment is half the battle when it comes to party preparation. A freezer is obviously essential for large-scale entertaining, so too is a food processor for chopping, grinding and slicing in large quantities. An electric mincer cuts pâté preparation time down to minutes rather than hours, and mixers and blenders are a boon for taking all the hard work out of beating, whipping and puréeing, etc. Electric carving knives and slicing machines are wonderful for accurate portion control – incredibly important when catering for many.

Equipment for making tea and coffee mustn't be overlooked on this sort of occasion, as your own family percolator or teapot simply won't be able to cope when everyone wants refreshing hot drinks before they go home. Work out quantities (see p. 130) and how you will organise the provision of this number of drinks.

SETTING THE TABLE

Arranging a buffet table correctly is all-important when catering for large numbers. It should not only look attractive, but should be laid out in such a way as to cause minimum inconvenience to your guests. Arrange the table so that guests can move easily around it, progressing naturally from plates and cutlery to the main dishes and the side dishes (see right). If desserts are included on the same table, put them where they can be reached after other dishes are cleared away.

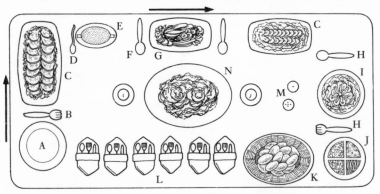

A	Plates	H	Salad servers
B	Serving fork	I	Salad bowl
C	Main dish	J	Pickles and relishes
D	Sauce ladle	K	Roll basket
E	Sauce boat	L	Napkins and cutlery
F	Serving spoon	M	Salt and pepper
G	Vegetable dish	N	Centrepiece and candles

CATERING QUANTITIES

APPROXIMATE QUANTITIES FOR BUFFET PARTIES

	1 portion	24–26 portions	Notes
Cheese (for biscuits)	25–40 g (1–1½ oz)	700–900 g (1½–2 lb) cheese plus 450 g (1 lb) butter 900 g (2 lb) biscuits	Allow the larger amounts for an assorted cheeseboard.
Cheese (for wine-and-cheese party)	75 g (3 oz)	2–2.3 kg (4½–5 lb) of at least 4 types	Buy more than this if serving a cheese dip.
Cooked meat	75–100 g (3–4 oz)	2.3–3 kg (5–6½ lb)	Half for stuffed cornets.
Fish cocktail: shrimp, prawn, tuna or crab	25 g (1 oz)	700 g (1½ lb) fish 2–3 lettuces 900 ml (1½ pints) sauce	In stemmed glasses, garnished with a shrimp or prawn.
Meat with bone boneless	150 g (5 oz) 75–100 g (3–4 oz)	3.2–3.6 kg (7–8 lb) 2.3–3 kg (5–6½ lb)	Cold roasts or barbecue chops. Casseroles, meat balls, sausages.
Pâté (for wine-and-pâté party)	75–100 g (3–4 oz)	2.3–3 kg (5–6½ lb)	Half for a starter.
Poultry: turkey chicken	75–100 g (3–4 oz) (boneless) 1 joint (150–225 g [5–8 oz])	7 kg (16 lb) (dressed) Six 1.1–1.4kg (2½–3lb) birds (dressed)	Serve hot or cold.
Rice or pasta	35 g (1½ oz) (uncooked)	900 g (2 lb)	Cook a day ahead, reheat in boiling water
Salad vegetables lettuce cucumber tomatoes boiled potatoes	⅙ 2.5 cm (1 inch) 1–2 50 g (2 oz)	3–4 2 cucumbers 1.3 kg (3 lb) 1.3 kg (3 lb)	Dress at last minute. For potato salads.
Sauces: French dressing	300 ml (½ pint) 12 portions	450–600 ml (¾–1 pint) 20 portions	Practical points Make in a lidded container and shake together just before serving.
Mayonnaise	600 ml (1 pint) 12 portions	900 ml–1 litre (1½–1¾ pint) 20 portions	
Soups: cream, clear or iced	200 ml (⅓ pint)	4.75 litres (1 gallon)	Serve garnished in mugs or cups.

SAVOURIES AND SWEETS

	Ingredients	Portions	Notes
Cheese straws	225 g (8 oz) cheese pastry	100 cheese straws	225 g (8 oz) flour, 100 g (4 oz) fat, 100 g (4 oz) cheese.
Cream (single or double)	50 ml (2 fl oz) 1 portion	1.1 litres (2 pints) 25 portions	To lighten and extend well chilled double cream, add 15 ml (1 tbsp) milk to each 142-ml (5-fl oz) carton cream before whipping. 142 ml (5 fl oz) cream, whipped, gives about 12 individual whirls.
Fruit salad	3 kg (6½ lb) fruit (3–4 pints) sugar syrup 900 ml (1½ pints) cream	25	Can be prepared a day ahead but bananas should be added just before serving.
Ice cream	2 family-sized blocks 12 portions	2.3 litres (4 pints) 12 portions	Keep at ice cube compartment temperature for easy serving.
Jelly	3 litres (2½ quarts)	25	
Meringues	6 egg whites 350 g (12 oz) caster sugar 450 ml (15 fl oz) whipped cream	50 (small) meringue halves	Sandwich meringue halves together with the whipped cream not more than 2 hours before serving.
Sausage rolls	700 g (1½ lb) shortcrust or flaky pastry 1 kg (2 lb) sausage meat	25–30 medium or 50 small rolls	Pastry based on 700 g (1½ lb) flour, 350–450 g (12 oz–1 lb) fat.

GIVING A DINNER PARTY

Giving a dinner party should be a pleasure, not a chore. If you go about it in the right way, your guests will feel at ease from the moment they walk through the front door, and you, too, will enjoy their company unflustered and unflapped.

Having carefully chosen your guests, and telephoned them or issued invitations well ahead (see right), the next step is to choose the menu and plan both the shopping and which dishes can be cooked in advance. Make lists of everything that has to be done and of the food and wine that has to be bought. Take account of the time you will have available for shopping and of any ingredients that will need to be ordered well ahead. Remember that many ingredients will store well in the freezer if necessary.

Table settings should be planned in accordance with your menu (see page 136). However simple, make the table setting both eye-catching and practical – however beautiful it is before everyone sits down, it must also work well, in an uncluttered way, while your guests are eating. On the day of the party, the table can be laid, in the morning, or whenever you have time to spare. When the table is ready, close the door to keep out any children and pets.

As your guests arrive, put them at their ease by offering them an aperitif. Make sure that everyone is relaxed (with a full glass) before you return to the kitchen to check on any last-minute cooking. If two of you are giving the dinner party, organise your duties well in advance – one of you should be in charge of the drinks (including serving wine with the meal), while the other sees to the food. If you are giving a dinner party on your own, ask one of your guests to help you out with the drinks.

INVITATIONS

Impromptu entertaining, while fun, can also be nerve-racking. Things will be much easier all round if parties are planned ahead. Two weeks is probably ample as far as your own preparations are concerned, but more time will be required if you are to find the right people free on the right date: three to four weeks for an average-sized party, at least four weeks for a larger party, and six weeks for events such as wedding receptions.

Invitations to informal dinner parties are normally made by telephone, but for large formal parties, most people find it easier to send out invitations – either on hand-written notes or cards, or the printed kind on which the details are filled in by hand (see right). Specially printed cards must be sent out for formal occasions, and will have to be ordered well in advance. Keep a list of the people you have invited and check them off as they reply.

Make things easier for your guests by including the following points on your invitations.

- A note at the bottom that says RSVP, and your telephone number.
- A mention not only of the time and place, but also the type of party it will be, such as 'Buffet Supper' or 'Lunch'. (An invitation to 'Sherry' or 'Cocktails' automatically assumes that only small cocktail snacks will be served.)

You're invited to a dinner party
at 8 Woodstock Terrace
on 21st December
time 8.30 p.m.
telephone 4306782

RSVP

MENU PLANNING

When planning a dinner party menu, it is important to be aware of your guests' likes and dislikes, to be realistic about your abilities as a cook and your kitchen's capabilities, and to have plenty of time to spend with your guests.

Whatever your menu, it should contain three or more well-balanced courses. The 'wet and dry' rule is a good one to follow when planning actual dishes; that is, a 'wet' course such as a soup or casserole should precede a 'dry' one such as a grilled steak or an apple tart. Aim, too, for balance in 'weight' of the courses. A thick soup with dumplings, followed by

steak pie and a steamed dessert may be traditional English fare, but is far too filling for all but the heartiest of appetites.

Flavour balance is the next part of the equation to consider. This is easily achieved by serving fish for one of the first two courses and meat or a meat-based dish (such as pâté) as the other. Similarly, one course based on a vegetable or fruit (such as avocado pear or melon), and one based on meat or fish makes a well-balanced combination. Fruit puddings go well with most menus, but avoid creamy desserts if either of the preceding courses has been served with a cream sauce. If fruit was served in either of the first courses, it is best to choose an alternative such as a chocolate-based recipe for the dessert.

Colour is important in menu planning, too. Unless you are specifically aiming for an effect of all one colour, aim for a pretty but complementary mix of colours in the food you serve. This can be achieved both through the recipes and their ingredients and with the help of garnishes and decorations.

Last but not least, plan the menu so that you leave plenty of time to be with your guests. A dish that needs very careful timing, such as a steak or Chicken Kiev, for example, will not allow for the fact that guests may not be punctual, or that people linger over their food longer than you had originally anticipated.

TIPS FOR A SUCCESSFUL DINNER PARTY

● Plan well ahead, down to the last detail.

● Prepare everything as much in advance as possible. Even fresh vegetables and salads can be prepared and put into poly-thene bags in the refrigerator.

● Leave time to relax and enter-tain your guests properly.

● Keep place settings pretty but not over-elaborate.

● Make sure guests have all the necessary plates and cutlery.

● Keep the lighting soft and subtle.

● Make sure you have enough ice for drinks.

● Eat away – but not too far away – from the kitchen.

● Make full use of sideboards and side-tables to save clutter and legwork.

● Don't panic if things go wrong – keep smiling and improvise – your guests will never know!

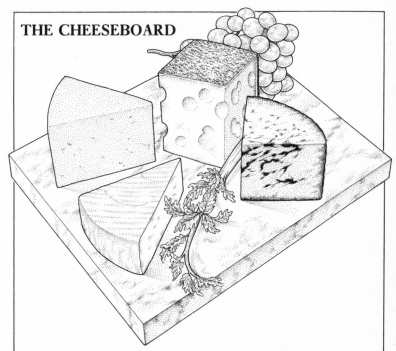

THE CHEESEBOARD

At an informal dinner party, a cheeseboard and fresh fruit can be served in place of a dessert. At a more formal dinner party, how-ever, cheese should be served as an extra course *in addition* to the dessert. Though usually served in the traditional English way after the dessert, it is also accept-able to serve it like the French do, before the dessert.

If buying cheese for a party several days in advance, take ac-count of the degree to which it will mature before it is served, particularly if you are choosing cheeses such as Brie or Camem-bert which are only at their best for a short period. Store cheese wrapped in cling film in the re-frigerator, unless you want it to ripen at room temperature, but always remove it from the re-frigerator and unwrap it at least 1 hour before serving. As well as bringing out the flavour, this will prevent the cheese from sweating unattractively when it is served.

A really good cheeseboard will contain a generous selection of different cheeses both for visual appeal and in order to cater for a wide range of tastes. Include mild cheeses such as Caerphilly, Wens-leydale or Gruyère, blue-veined cheeses such as Stilton or Dolce-latte or the less powerful new English Lymeswold; soft and pungent cheeses such as Brie or Camembert, a robust Cheddar or Leicester and perhaps a sharp-flavoured cheese such as Sage Derby or a soft French Boursin. Goat's or sheep's milk cheese also adds interest.

To accompany the cheese, serve a selection of crackers and biscuits, plus some rolls or French bread, since many people prefer these as an accompaniment to strongly flavoured cheeses. Butter should also be offered. Sticks of crisp celery and fresh fruit such as grapes can either be arranged on the cheeseboard itself or served separately.

If you wish, provide guests with a fork as well as a knife so that they can eat their cheese on its own. On the cheeseboard itself, provide at least one cheese knife for serving, and more if the board contains cheeses with very well-defined flavours.

PREPARING THE TABLE

SEATING YOUR GUESTS

Seat guests at a dinner party so that, as far as possible, men and women are placed alternately round the table. Husbands and wives should be near, but not directly opposite, each other. Host and hostess should always sit at opposite ends of a rectangular table or opposite each other at a round table, even if this upsets the alternate man/woman arrangement. The chief female guest should sit to the right of the host, the chief male guest to the right of the hostess. The diagram below shows an ideal seating arrangement for few people.

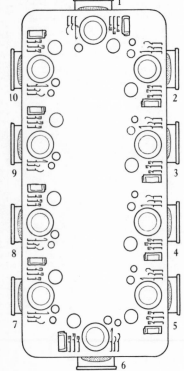

1 Host; 2 Second woman; 3 Man; 4 Woman; 5 Chief male guest; 6 Hostess; 7 Second man; 8 Woman; 9 Man; 10 Chief female guest.

LAYING THE TABLE

When laying each place setting at the table (see below), arrange the knives and forks so that they are used from the outside inwards.

Knife blades should always face inwards. The dessert spoon and fork should be placed above, so that the handle of the dessert spoon points towards the knife blades. For a formal dinner party, arrange the napkin on the side plate to the left of the setting, or in a napkin ring to the right. For an informal setting, the napkin can be simply placed on the centre plate if wished. Arrange glasses for water and wine above the knives. Finish your table decorations with a central flower arrangement. Candles should be placed equidistant from the table ends or placed in a pretty group at the table centre.

NAPKINS

A dinner table is set off to perfection by a fine tablecloth and decoratively folded napkins. Ideally, the napkins should be of starched linen or other good-quality material, in a colour that matches or contrasts with that of the tablecloth, but you can use good-quality, thick paper napkins as a reasonable substitute.

Napkins can be simply folded into triangles or rectangles, and look wonderful housed in decorative napkin rings of either traditional or modern design.

Another way of adding a decorative and impressive touch to the dinner table is by folding napkins into shapes such as the ones shown on these pages.

WATERLILY

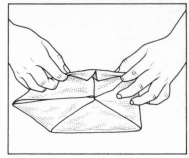

1 Lay starched napkin out flat, fold all four points into the centre. Then repeat this same procedure twice more.

2 When this has been done, turn the napkin over, then fold the four points into the centre again.

3 Holding the centre of the napkin very firmly with the fingers of one hand, use your other hand to unfold a 'petal' from beneath each of the four corners of the napkin as shown.

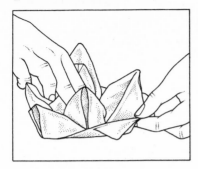

4 Carefully pull out four more petals between the original ones in the same way.

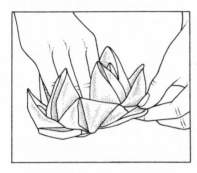

5 The waterlily should now have eight points. Then pull out four petals from beneath the original four as in steps 3 and 4.

6 The completed waterlily now has twelve points, as shown in the illustration above.

BISHOP'S HAT

For this type of fold, the napkin need not be stiffly starched.

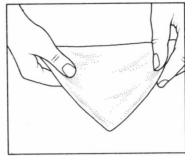

1 Fold the napkin into four to make a square shape. Take the point where the two folded sides meet to a point just above the centre of the square.

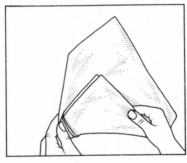

2 Turn the napkin over, then fold back the two sides of the napkin so that they overlap.

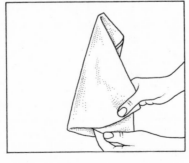

3 Tuck the point of one side into the pocket on the other side. Stand the completed 'bishop's hat' napkin on its base.

BUTTERFLY

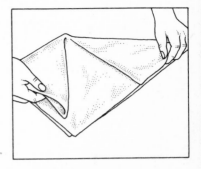

1 Lay starched napkin out flat, fold in half diagonally to make a triangle with point facing upwards. Fold point at bottom right-hand corner up to tip of triangle; fold bottom left-hand corner up to apex.

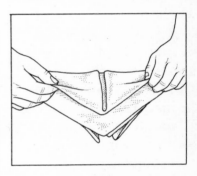

2 Turn this diamond shape over, keeping a firm hold on the loose points, then fold opposite points of the diamond upward to create a triangle.

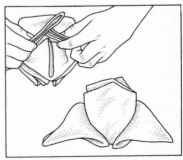

3 Tuck the left-hand corner firmly inside the right hand one. Stand the napkin up on its end, then turn down free pieces at the sides to form the 'wings'.

Drinks

When entertaining friends and relatives, whether it's a roomful at a wedding reception or just a couple at a dinner party, the choosing and serving of drinks is just as important as the food. In this chapter we take you through all the drinks you should ever have to serve – from aperitifs, wine and Champagne, right through to cups and punches, after–dinner port and liqueurs, and even coffee.

APERITIFS

Before dinner, it is customary to serve an aperitif or appetiser, with 'nibbles' or canapés. The aperitif may be a traditional drink such as sherry – dry, sweet or amontillado as you prefer – or a 'standard' spirit-based drink such as gin or vodka and tonic, or whisky with soda or dry ginger.

Other possibilities are drinks flavoured with aromatic herbs such as Campari (with ice, soda and a slice of orange), and the many types of vermouth. Vermouth may be served on its own with ice and lemon or orange, made into a long drink with tonic or mineral water or used to spark up gin or vodka.

You can also make a huge variety of cocktails. For a professional touch, try 'frosting' cocktail glasses with sugar or salt: first dip the rims in very lightly beaten egg white, then dip them in sugar or salt and leave them for several hours to dry.

Other aperitifs include Champagne and drinks more often served after dinner, such as port or Madeira, usually served chilled in this case.

WINE

Good wine is the perfect complement to good food, but there is a great deal of mystique surrounding the subject of which wines should be served with particular foods.

The cardinal rule used to be that white wine should accompany the first course or fish or chicken, and that red wines were for serving with red meat and game. A sweet wine, it was decreed, should accompany the dessert course. Nowadays, however, it is much more important to consider the taste and 'weight' of the food you are serving and to choose your wines accordingly. A light food such as fish needs an equally light wine, while 'heavier' dishes such as casseroles need richer, more full-bodied wines. While white wines certainly go well with light starters and have an acidity which offsets the flavour of fish perfectly, a young, light-bodied red wine will do just as well; similarly, a full-bodied white wine, such as a white Burgundy can be as good with a beef casserole or game pie as a rich red. A sweet wine is, of course, needed for desserts. See our chart below.

WINE WITH FOOD

First courses (not soups), salads, cold meats: Any dry to medium white wine, but particularly Muscadet, Chablis, Pouilly Fumé

Soups: Sherry, Madeira, any dry white wine or light dry red wine but particularly dry Sauternes, Graves

Fish: Any light dry or medium white wine or a light red, particularly Muscadet, Mosel, Meursault, Chablis, Hermitage Blanc, Alsace

Red meat, game: Any sturdy, full-bodied red, particularly Bordeaux, Chianti, Barolo, Côtes du Rhône, Valpolicella, Médoc, St Emilion

White meat (not stuffed or served with heavy sauce): Any full-bodied white or a medium-bodied red, particularly Chianti Classico, Riesling

Cheese: Port, or a young red wine such as Beaujolais Nouveau

Dessert: Any sweet white wine, particularly Asti Spumante, sweet Sauternes, Vouvray, Marsala, Sweet Muscatel

---

*These are, of course, only guidelines. Do not be afraid to experiment and take advantage of special offers and bin ends when out wine shopping, or if you order wine by mail order. Equally, make use of friends' recommendations.

CUPS AND PUNCHES

Fruit cups and punches make a refreshing change from wine in hot weather and are also a good way of catering for large numbers. Try some of the following recipes, or serve a drink such as Pimms No. 1, a gin-based drink served with fizzy lemonade or half lemonade and half sparkling mineral water, topped with orange and lemon slices and mint sprigs.

MULLED WINE

Serves about 8

600 ml (1 pint) water
225 g (8 oz) sugar
8 cloves
1 stick of cinnamon
4 lemons, thinly sliced
2 bottles burgundy or claret
2 oranges or lemons, thinly sliced, to decorate

1 Bring the water, sugar, cloves and cinnamon to the boil. Add the lemons, stir and leave to stand for 10 minutes.

2 Pour back into the saucepan and add the burgundy or claret. Heat but do not boil.

3 Strain the wine into a bowl and serve hot, decorated with the orange or lemon slices.

CHAMPAGNE CUP

Serves about 8

large piece of ice
25 ml (1½ tbsp) apricot brandy
25 ml (1½ tbsp) orange-flavoured liqueur
50 ml (2 fl oz) brandy
1 bottle Champagne, chilled
1 'split' soda water
fruit, to decorate

Put the ice in a large jug and add the ingredients in the order given. Stir well and decorate with slices of fruit in season. Serve at once.

FRUIT PUNCH

Serves about 20

2 bottles of dry white wine
2 bottles of red wine
90 ml (6 tbsp) orange-flavoured liqueur
2 eating apples, cored and sliced
pieces of melon
orange slices, quartered
few strawberries
crushed ice
1.7 litres (3 pints) fizzy lemonade

Pour the wines and liqueur over the fruit and ice in a bowl. Chill, then add the lemonade. Serve at once, while ice-cold.

APPLE PUNCH

Serves 8–10

2 red-skinned eating apples
2 large oranges
286 ml (10 fl oz) apple juice
1.1 litres (2 pints) soda water
1.1 litres (2 pints) dry ginger ale

1 Rub the apples with a clean dry tea towel; quarter, core and slice. Slice the oranges into small pieces, discarding the pips.

2 Place the apple juice and prepared fruits into a large bowl, cover and chill for about 2 hours. Chill the bottles of soda water and ginger ale.

3 Just before serving, measure out the soda water and ginger ale and combine with the apple juice. Ladle into glasses for serving.

KIR

Makes 1 serving

4 parts dry white wine
1 part blackcurrant-flavoured liqueur

Thoroughly chill the wine before combining it with the liqueur; serve in a claret glass.

OPENING A CHAMPAGNE BOTTLE

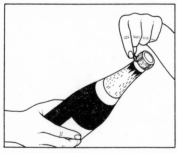

1 Hold the Champagne bottle in one hand, and remove the wire muzzle around the top of the bottle with the other.

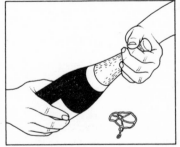

2 Slightly tilt the bottle and hold the cork firmly, rotating the bottle at the same time.

3 Pull the bottle down gently and slowly to reduce internal pressure. The cork will come out with a soft 'pop'. Wipe rim.

AFTER DINNER DRINKS

After dinner, when your guests are relaxed and ready for their coffee, is the time when you should offer brandy, liqueurs or port. These are by no means obligatory, but they do make a wonderful end to a dinner party meal.

If you only have the resources to choose one after-dinner drink, then brandy or port are always safe options. Some brandies are given a star rating (5 star being the best), but this is not standard. VSOP (Very Special Old Pale) means that a brandy has matured for at least 5 years. The names cognac and armagnac mean that the wines from which the brandy was made come from these specific wine-growing regions.

BRANDY AND LIQUEUR GLASSES

Serve brandy in a large, balloon-shaped glass. The drinker can then swirl the brandy around as it warms with the heat of the hands, thus allowing the aroma to develop.

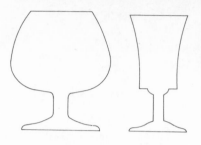

Liqueurs should be served in small glasses – either wide-rimmed or taller, with parallel sides and a shape like a sherry glass.

PORT

Port is a drink surrounded with traditions and customs. Vintage port, which takes 15–20 years to mature, should always be decanted through a muslin filter before it is drunk, as should crusted port which is port treated as a vintage but not actually made in a vintage year. Other ports do not need this treatment. Ports which are ready to drink without decanting can be ruby, tawny or white. Ruby port is rich and red, but does not have the subtle maturity of a tawny port. White port is made from white grapes.

COFFEE

Coffee makes a perfect finale to a dinner party, and it is customary for guests to retire to comfortable chairs, away from the table, to drink it (with brandy or liqueurs if liked), but if the conversation is flowing freely it may seem best for guests to have a first serving of coffee at the table rather than to break up the flow of 'chat'.

Fresh coffee can be bought as beans or ready-ground. If you do not have your own coffee grinder it is best to buy the beans, then have them ground to the coarseness you prefer in the shop. Whatever the type of coffee you choose (see box) you should ensure it is as fresh as possible, that is, it is purchased from a reputable coffee merchant or other reliable outlet which has a fast turnover – good coffee merchants roast their beans on a daily basis. Unground beans will keep their freshly roasted flavour for up to two weeks in an airtight tin, but ground coffee will only keep for 7–10 days, even in an airtight tin in the refrigerator. Beans will keep for 4–5 months and ground coffee for 4–5 weeks in the freezer.

TYPES OF LIQUEUR

There are so many flavours of liqueurs to choose from that the selection must, in the last analysis, be a personal one. The following are some of the most popular, described with their predominant flavours:

Advocaat: eggs (or alcoholic egg custard!)
Amaretto: apricots and almonds
Anisette: aniseed
Aquavit: schnapps (potato or grain spirit) flavoured with caraway or dill
Bénédictine: herby liqueur in a brandy base
Calvados: apple brandy
Cassis: blackcurrant
Chartreuse: herbs – the yellow is less strong than the green
Cointreau: bitter orange peel
Crème de menthe: mint

Curaçao: bitter orange
Drambuie: whisky, herbs and (perhaps) heather honey
Galliano: yellow Italian herb liqueur
Grand Marnier: orange-flavoured, based on cognac
Kahlua: strong Mexican coffee-flavoured liqueur
Kummel: caraway
Maraschino: cherries
Ouzo: Greek aniseed liqueur
Royal Mint Chocolate: peppermint and chocolate
Southern Comfort: American whisky-based liqueur with oranges, other fruits and herbs
Strega: combination of over 70 herbs and barks in a sweetish liqueur
Tia Maria: Blue mountain coffee, spices and rum

TYPES OF COFFEE

These are the types of coffee suitable for a dinner party:
After-dinner: usually a blend of strong-flavoured, dark-roasted beans.
Blue-Mountain blend: a mixture of coffees, probably including some Jamaican.
Brazilian: smooth and mild when at its best. A good choice for any occasion.
Chagga: a medium to dark roast coffee with a rich flavour, originating in Tanzania.
Java: an unusual, strong, dark roast coffee best served black as after-dinner coffee.
Kenya: a medium roast with a distinctive aromatic quality.
Mysore: a rich strong coffee from southern India.

MAKING COFFEE

The best coffee is made with freshly roasted and ground beans and with freshly boiled water. As a rule, allow 25 g (1 oz) coffee per 300 ml ($\frac{1}{2}$ pint) water. This is also about the amount you should allow per guest.

However you make coffee, it should *never* be allowed to boil, since this ruins the flavour. The following are the most successful methods:

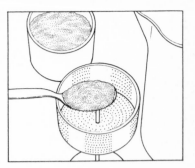

Filter methods (above and below): in these methods, hot water passes through a filter paper containing finely ground coffee beans. There are many versions of this method, many incorporating electrical devices to keep the made coffee warm.

Percolator method: water is brought to the boil in the percolator and forced over coffee grounds in a basket in its top. Although electric percolators have a timing device, there is a risk of the coffee becoming 'stewed'.

Cona or syphon method: a special coffee maker in which boiling water is forced from a lower container into an upper container in which medium-ground coffee is placed. When the coffee maker is removed from the heat the prepared coffee flows down into the lower container again, from which it is served.

Saucepan method: the water and coarsely ground coffee are placed in a saucepan and brought almost to boiling point. They are infused over a very low heat for 5 minutes, then strained into a warm jug.

SERVING COFFEE

Serve after-dinner coffee in small cups. If guests prefer 'white' coffee, use cold milk or thin cream, *never* boiled milk. Offer demerara sugar or special coffee sugar crystals as a sweetener.

Jug method: medium-ground coffee beans are placed in a warmed jug and boiling water poured over them. After 4–5 minutes' infusion, the coffee is strained straight into the cups or into a clean, warm jug. There is a more sophisticated version of the jug method marketed as *La Cafe-tière* (above). The coffee jug contains strainer which is plunged through the coffee before serving.

IRISH COFFEE

1 Warm as many goblets as needed, then put 1 measure of whisky and 1 teaspoon light soft brown sugar in each.

2 Pour in piping hot coffee to come about 2.5 cm (1 inch) from the top.

3 Pour double cream over the back of a teaspoon into the glass. The cream will float on top.

Use other liqueurs to make the following coffees:
Rum (Caribbean coffee)
Kirsch (German coffee)
Calvados (Normandy coffee)
Tia Maria (Calypso coffee)
Strega (Witch's coffee)
Cointreau and Curaçao can also be used, if wished.

Presenting the Food

One of the secrets of successful entertaining is knowing how to present the food you have so carefully cooked in the most attractive way. And this doesn't mean that you have to be an expert at piping, or a whizz with aspic!
This chapter is packed with ideas for garnishing and decorating, all of which are stunningly effective, yet amazingly simple to do.

GARNISHES

Add a professional touch to your cooking by using some of the savoury garnishes suggested on these pages. The garnishes can simply be placed on the dish or, if the dish in question is already covered with a layer of aspic, can themselves be fixed in position with aspic. To do this, simply dip the prepared garnishes in aspic and set them in position, then, when they are well set, cover the entire dish with another aspic layer.

Garnishes and decorations should, as a rule, be edible; they should also look fresh and shiny, not stale and dull. This fresh effect can be enhanced by the use of aspic or a sweet jelly, both on the dish itself, or as part of the garnish. Here are a few ideas for attractive garnishes and decorations.

SPRING ONION TASSELS

1 Remove the base and most of the green part from each of the spring onions.

2 Make several parallel slits from the top of each onion to within about 2.5 cm (1 inch) of the base.

3 Allow the onions to stand in a bowl of iced water for about 1 hour to curl, then drain well before using.

LEMON TWISTS

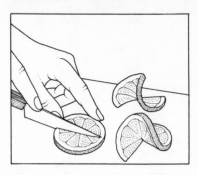

Cut thin slices of lemon. Make a cut to the centre of each slice then twist into an S-shape. A sprig of parsley or another herb may be placed at the centre of the twist for extra colour. This method can also be used with orange, lime or cucumber slices.

CELERY FRILLS

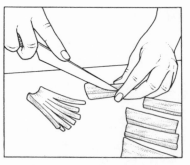

1 Cut sticks of celery into pieces about 7.5 cm (3 inches) long. Make parallel cuts in each end of the celery about 2.5 cm (1 inch) deep, then flatten out the celery.

2 At each end, make a careful cut into the 'teeth', so that the teeth are cut in half lengthways.

3 Leave the prepared sticks of celery in iced water for about 1 hour so that the frill can curl up.

TOMATO WHIRLS

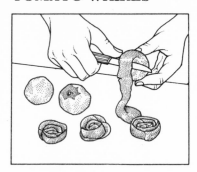

1 Using a small sharp knife, cut the skin and a very thin layer of flesh from a tomato, starting at the top and working round in the way that you would peel an orange.

2 Trim the ends of the peel neatly, then curl it up so that it forms a flower shape. Secure with a toothpick until ready to use.

RADISH ROSES

1 Trim each radish. Starting at the top of the radish, make rows of small cuts into the radish flesh to make petals. The number of rows will depend on the size of the radish.

2 Place the prepared radishes in a bowl of iced water for about 1 hour so that the 'petals' open out to form a rose.

VANDYKING ORANGES

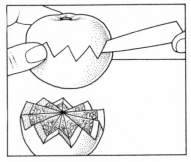

1 Using a small, thin-bladed knife, make a slantwise cut in the equator of an orange to the centre.

2 Without removing the knife, make a series of zig-zag cuts all round the equator of the fruit. Gently twist the two halves apart.

This can also be used on tomatoes, grapefruit, lemons or similar savoury garnishes.

FLUTED OR 'TURNED' MUSHROOMS

1 Choose firm, white button mushrooms. Hold a small sharp knife with the blade parallel to the mushroom stalk.

2 Keeping your thumb and fingers well away from the blade, turn the mushroom against the knife so that thin, curved strips of the mushroom skin are removed evenly all round.

MIMOSA EGGS

Separate the egg yolks from the whites of hard-boiled eggs. Chop the whites finely then sieve the yolks. The sieved yolk can also be formed into small balls to look like mimosa flowers.

GHERKIN FANS

Make parallel cuts in gherkins to within about 1 cm ($\frac{1}{2}$ inch) of the base. Open out into a fan shape.

CUCUMBER WHEELS

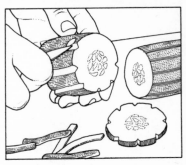

Using a sharp knife, remove thin strips of skin evenly from all round a cucumber. Then cut into slices.

DECORATIONS

Effective decorations for sweet dishes range from the stunningly simple to the sophistication of piped cream or icing. Even if you are not an experienced cook, you can try some of the suggestions shown here.

PASTRY TASSELS

Cut out a strip of pastry about 10 cm (4 inches) long and 2.5 cm (1 inch) wide. Make parallel cuts along the strip to end about 0.5 cm ($\frac{1}{4}$ inch) from the edge. Roll up the pastry, stand it on its end and fan out the cut edge. Insert into centre hole in pastry-topped pies.

CRUSHED CARAMEL

Slowly dissolve 75 g (3 oz) sugar in 75 ml (3 fl oz) water over gentle heat, then increase the heat and boil until the liquid has turned to a rich caramel colour. Pour the mixture immediately into a shallow baking tin lined with waxed paper. Leave to set. Crush caramel with a rolling pin. Use over desserts.

MARZIPAN 'ORANGES'

Colour batches of marzipan with orange and green food colouring. With your fingers, shape small amounts of the orange marzipan into balls. Stick a trimmed whole clove in the end for the 'eye' of the fruit. Roll on the fine side of a conical or box grater to give the texture of orange skin, then roll in caster sugar. Attach 'leaves' made from the green-coloured marzipan. Use on cakes, or as petits fours or presents in sweet cases.

CHOCOLATE CARAQUE

Melt chocolate in a double boiler or a bowl over a pan of hot water, then pour and spread on to a cold surface (ideally a marble slab) and leave until just on the point of setting. Push the blade of a large knife away from you at an angle to make curls. Use to decorate cakes, mousses and soufflés.

For a less dramatic, though simpler, version of caraque, make chocolate curls: shave a bar of chilled chocolate with a vegetable peeler or cannelle knife.

FROSTED FRUITS AND FLOWERS

Whisk together the white of 1 egg with 2 teaspoonfuls of cold water to give a frothy mixture. Brush the mixture on to fruits or flowers, then dip these in caster sugar. Shake off any excess, then spread out on greaseproof paper and leave in the air to dry for at least 24 hours. Use to decorate cakes, mousses and soufflés.

CITRUS JULIENNE

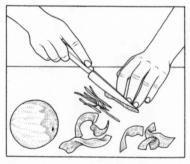

Remove very thin strips of rind from citrus fruit with a cannelle knife or vegetable peeler, making sure that the strips contain no traces of pith. Blanch the strips in boiling water for about 3 minutes, then drain and rinse under cold running water. Dry thoroughly and cut into julienne strips about 0.5 cm ($\frac{1}{4}$ inch) thick and about 5 cm (2 inches) long. Use to sprinkle over desserts; looks especially good on rosettes of whipped cream or buttercream icing.

CHOCOLATE LEAVES

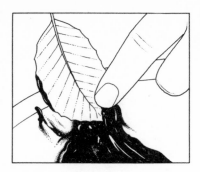

1 Melt the chocolate in a double boiler or a bowl over a pan of hot water.

2 Using rose leaves which have been thoroughly washed and dried, drag the upper surface of each leaf through the chocolate, making sure that the underside of the leaf does not become chocolate-coated too.

3 Turn the leaves chocolate-side up and place on greaseproof paper to set. When the chocolate has set, carefully peel off the leaf.

FLOWER DESIGNS

1 Make up some very firm jelly of the colour you wish and use aspic cutters or a sharp knife to make petal shapes.

2 Construct flowers – using the jelly petals, angelica strips for stems and silver dragees for the centres. Whole blanched almonds can be alternated with the jelly in the flowers.

Arrange the shapes on the top or around the edges just before serving. The jelly flowers will keep in the refrigerator for 2–3 days. Store in an airtight container.

PIPED CREAM

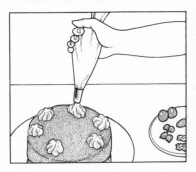

Whip double cream until stiff but not cheesy in texture then, using a piping bag and a star nozzle, pipe rosettes of cream around a dessert or cake and top each one with a nut, cherry or some other kind of fruit. Or sprinkle with grated chocolate, toasted chopped nuts or toasted desiccated coconut.

ICING SUGAR PATTERNS

1 Place a patterned paper doily, or a template you have cut yourself, on a cake (or get someone to help by holding it just above the surface of a delicate cake or dessert).

2 Sift over icing sugar – the pattern of holes will be reproduced on the surface of the cake or dessert.

Chocolate powder can be used in a similar way on a lightly coloured cake.

COLOUR MATCHES

Here are some ideas for using colour matches in food and their decorations: they should set you thinking to try some colour combinations of your own.

Red, white and green as in tomatoes, Mozzarella and avocado

Black, white and yellow as in hard-boiled eggs topped with lumpfish roe

Pink, black and green as in ham cornets stuffed with cream cheese and spinach and garnished with black olives

Biege, green and yellow as in veal, fish or chicken with cucumber and lemon twists

Strong colours with pale ones such as a salad of grated raw beetroot, carrot and celeriac

Shades of orange as in orange mousse with pale orange cream rosettes topped with julienne orange strips

Brown and purple as in chocolate cake with frosted African violets

Orange and green as in carrots with chopped fresh tarragon leaves

Pale yellow and dark red as in lemon souffle decorated with blackberries

Light brownish yellow and **deep purple** as in rolled up filled dessert pancakes with blackcurrant sauce

Celebration Cakes

Don't be daunted by the idea of making a celebration cake, you'll find it one of the most rewarding things you've ever done. It may not be quite so perfect as the professionals do it, but you'll find there's so much more satisfaction in making and decorating a cake yourself – and in seeing the pleasure such a cake brings to those who receive it.

MAKING A CELEBRATION CAKE

A rich fruit cake improves with keeping so can be made from 2–3 months in advance. After cooling and soaking with brandy, wrap the cake in greaseproof paper and then in a double thickness of foil. If you wish, a little more brandy may be poured over halfway through the storing period. Store in an airtight tin in a cool, dry place.

TIERED CAKES
When you are planning a wedding cake, choose the sizes of the tiers carefully, avoiding a combination that would look too heavy. Good proportions for a three-tier cake are 30.5, 23 and 15 cm (12, 9 and 6 inch); for a two-tier cake 30.5 and 20.5 cm (12 and 8 inch) or 25.5 and 15 cm (10 and 6 inch). The bottom tier should be deeper than the upper ones, therefore cakes of 25.5–30.5 cm (10–12 inch) diameter are generally made about 7.5 cm (3 inch) deep, while those 18–23 cm (7–9 inch) are 6.5 cm (2½ inch) deep and 12.5–15 cm (5–6 inches) are 5 cm (2 inches) deep.

Don't attempt to make the bigger sizes of cake unless you have a really large oven, as you should allow at least 2.5 cm (1 inch) space between the oven walls and the tin. For a three-tier cake, bake the two smaller ones together and the largest one separately.

You can expect to cut 8–10 portions of cake from each 450 g (1 lb) cooked mixture.

Cake boards
Silver is the usual colour (except for a Golden Wedding cake). The board should be 5 cm (2 inches) larger than the cake, for example, for a 20.5-cm (8-inch) cake use a 25.5-cm (10-inch) board. For a very large cake use a board 4 cm (1½ inches) bigger than the cake.

RICH FRUIT CAKE

1 Weigh the ingredients for size of cake you wish to make (see chart opposite). Grease and line the appropriate-sized cake tin, using a double thickness of grease-proof paper, and tie a double band of brown paper round the outside.

2 Wash and dry fruit if necessary, and mix together in a large bowl. Add flaked almonds.

3 Sift flour and spices into another bowl with pinch of salt. Then put butter, sugar and lemon rind into a warmed mixing bowl and cream together until pale and fluffy.

4 Add beaten eggs, a little at a time, beating well after each addition. Fold flour into mixture; add brandy, then fruit and nuts.

5 Turn mixture into tin, spreading it evenly and making sure there are no air pockets. Make a hollow in the centre. Stand tin on several thicknesses of newspaper in the oven.

6 Bake in the oven at 150°C (300°F) mark 2 for the required time (see chart), until a fine skewer inserted in the centre comes out clean. (If cake is 25 cm (10 inches) or upwards, reduce heat to 130°C (250°F) mark ½ after two-thirds of cooking time.)

7 To prevent cake from over-browning, cover with grease-proof paper after about 1½ hours. When cooked, leave to cool in tin before turning out on to a wire rack. Prick top with a fine skewer and pour 30–45 ml (2–3 tbsp) brandy over it before storing.

8 Wrap the cake in greaseproof paper and then in a double thickness of foil and store in an airtight tin.

QUANTITIES AND SIZES FOR SQUARE AND ROUND CELEBRATION CAKES

If you want to make a formal cake, this chart shows you the amount of ingredients required to fill the chosen cake tin or tins.

SQUARE TIN SIZE	12.5 cm *(5 inch)*	15 cm *(6 inch)*	18 cm *(7 inch)*	20.5 cm *(8 inch)*	23 cm *(9 inch)*	25.5 cm *(10 inch)*	28 cm *(11 inch)*	30.5 cm *(12 inch)*
ROUND TIN SIZE	15 cm *(6 inch)*	18 cm *(7 inch)*	20.5 cm *(8 inch)*	23 cm *(9 inch)*	25.5 cm *(10 inch)*	28 cm *(11 inch)*	30.5 cm *(12 inch)*	33 cm *(13 inch)*
Currants	200 g *(7 oz)*	225 g *(8 oz)*	350 g *(12 oz)*	400 g *(14 oz)*	625 g *(22 oz)*	775 g *(28 oz)*	1.1 kg *(40 oz)*	1.5 kg *(52 oz)*
Sultanas	75 g *(3 oz)*	100 g *(3½ oz)*	125 g *(4½ oz)*	175 g *(6 oz)*	225 g *(8 oz)*	375 g *(13 oz)*	400 g *(14 oz)*	525 g *(19 oz)*
Raisins, seedless	75 g *(3 oz)*	100 g *(3½ oz)*	125 g *(4½ oz)*	175 g *(6 oz)*	225 g *(8 oz)*	375 g *(13 oz)*	400 g *(14 oz)*	525 g *(19 oz)*
Glacé cherries	50 g *(2 oz)*	50 g *(2 oz)*	75 g *(3 oz)*	125 g *(4½ oz)*	175 g *(6 oz)*	250 g *(9 oz)*	275 g *(10 oz)*	350 g *(12 oz)*
Mixed peel	25 g *(1 oz)*	25 g *(1 oz)*	50 g *(2 oz)*	75 g *(3 oz)*	100 g *(3½ oz)*	150 g *(5 oz)*	200 g *(7 oz)*	250 g *(9 oz)*
Flaked almonds	25 g *(1 oz)*	25 g *(1 oz)*	50 g *(2 oz)*	75 g *(3 oz)*	100 g *(3½ oz)*	150 g *(5 oz)*	200 g *(7 oz)*	250 g *(9 oz)*
Plain flour	150 g *(5 oz)*	175 g *(6 oz)*	200 g *(7 oz)*	300 g *(11 oz)*	400 g *(14 oz)*	600 g *(21 oz)*	700 g *(24 oz)*	825 g *(29 oz)*
Mixed spice	1.25 ml *(¼ tsp)*	1.25 ml *(¼ tsp)*	2.5 ml *(½ tsp)*	2.5 ml *(½ tsp)*	5 ml *(1 tsp)*	5 ml *(1 tsp)*	10 ml *(2 tsp)*	12.5 ml *(2½ tsp)*
Cinnamon	1.25 ml *(¼ tsp)*	1.25 ml *(¼ tsp)*	2.5 ml *(½ tsp)*	2.5 ml *(½ tsp)*	5 ml *(1 tsp)*	5 ml *(1 tsp)*	10 ml *(2 tsp)*	12.5 ml *(2½ tsp)*
Butter	125 g *(4½ oz)*	150 g *(5 oz)*	175 g *(6 oz)*	250 g *(9 oz)*	350 g *(12 oz)*	500 g *(18 oz)*	600 g *(21 oz)*	800 g *(28 oz)*
Sugar	125 g *(4½ oz)*	150 g *(5 oz)*	175 g *(6 oz)*	250 g *(9 oz)*	350 g *(12 oz)*	500 g *(18 oz)*	600 g *(21 oz)*	800 g *(28 oz)*
Lemon rind	a little	a little	a little	¼ lemon	¼ lemon	½ lemon	½ lemon	1 lemon
Large eggs, size 1 or 2	2	2½	3	4	6	9	11	14
Brandy	15 ml *(1 tbsp)*	15 ml *(1 tbsp)*	15–30 ml *(1–2 tbsp)*	30 ml *(2 tbsp)*	30–45 ml *(2–3 tbsp)*	45 ml *(3 tbsp)*	45 ml *(3 tbsp)*	60 ml *(4 tbsp)*
Time (approx)	2½ hours	2½–3 hours	3 hours	3½–4 hours	4 hours	5½ hours	7 hours	8 hours
Weight when cooked	900 g *(2 lb)*	1.4 kg *(2½ lb)*	1.6 kg *(3½ lb)*	2.2 kg *(4½ lb)*	2.7 kg *(6 lb)*	4 kg *(9 lb)*	5.2 kg *(11½ lb)*	6.7 kg *(15 lb)*

ASSEMBLING THE CAKE

You can either make your own almond paste (see below) or buy it ready made. Home-made is nicer but takes slightly longer to dry out. Buy ready made paste shortly before you want to use it and check that it's not old stock. The fresher it is, the more pliable it will be. You will also need some sieved apricot jam.

COUNTDOWN TO THE DAY

14–20 days before Apply the almond paste. You will find the quantity needed for the size of cake on the chart below. Loosely cover the cake and store in a cool, dry place for 4–5 days.

10–15 days before Apply the first coat of royal icing and leave to dry for 1–2 days, then apply the second coat, if necessary. The chart below gives the quantity of icing required for the size of cake.

8–12 days before Assemble or make all the separate decorations required for the cake.

7 days before Complete all further decorating a week before the cake is to be served. Do not assemble a tiered cake, however, until the very last possible moment.

APPLYING ALMOND PASTE

1 To cover a round or square cake, first measure round the cake with a piece of string. Dust your work surface liberally with icing sugar and roll out two thirds of the paste to a rectangle, half the length of the string and twice the depth of the cake.

2 Trim the edges neatly with a knife, then cut the rectangle in half lengthways. Brush the sides of the cake with apricot glaze. Hold a round cake on its side, between the palms of your hands, and roll it along the strips of paste.

3 For a square cake, position one side of the cake on half of one strip of paste, and fold the other half up to cover a second side. Repeat for the other two sides. Keep the top edge of the cake square with the almond paste. Smooth the joins with a palette knife and mould any surplus paste into the bottom edge of the cake.

4 Turn the cake bottom side up onto a board. Brush the flat top of the cake with apricot glaze. Roll out the remaining almond paste to a round or square the same size as the top of the cake.

5 Lift on to the top of the cake with the rolling pin. Lightly roll with the rolling pin, then smooth the join and leave to dry.

ALMOND PASTE

| 100 g (4 oz) icing sugar |
| 100 g (4 oz) caster sugar |
| 225 g (8 oz) ground almonds |
| 2.5 ml ($\frac{1}{2}$ tsp) vanilla flavouring |
| 15–30 ml (1–2 tbsp) lemon juice |
| 1 egg, grade 3 or 4, beaten |

1 Sift the icing sugar into a bowl and stir in the caster sugar and almonds.

2 Add the flavouring and 15 ml (1 tbsp) lemon juice then work in the egg with more lemon juice if needed to form a stiff paste. Form into a ball and knead lightly.

Makes about 450 g (1 lb). To calculate different quantities, see chart, below.

DECORATING A CHRISTMAS CAKE

After applying flat icing, leave to dry for 1–2 days. Then prepare decorations and leave to dry for 24 hours. For holly leaves, colour almond paste dark green. Roll out on non-stick paper.

| **almond paste (left)** |
| **green and red food colouring** |
| **silver balls and ribbon** |

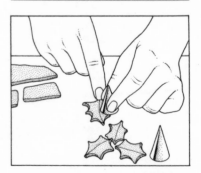

1 Cut into small rectangles, then into holly leaf shapes with base of an icing nozzle. Mark in centre vein with a knife and leave to dry.

Quantities of paste and icing to decorate a wedding cake

SQUARE CAKE	12.5 cm	15 cm	18 cm	20.5 cm	23 cm	25.5 cm	28 cm	30.5 cm
	(5 inch)	*(6 inch)*	*(7 inch)*	*(8 inch)*	*(9 inch)*	*(10 inch)*	*(11 inch)*	*(12 inch)*
ROUND CAKE	15 cm	18 cm	20.5 cm	23 cm	25.5 cm	28 cm	30.5 cm	33 cm
	(6 inch)	*(7 inch)*	*(8 inch)*	*(9 inch)*	*(10 inch)*	*(11 inch)*	*(12 inch)*	*(13 inch)*
Almond paste	350 g	450 g	550 g	800 g	900 g	1 kg	1.1 kg	1.4 kg
	(12 oz)	*(1 lb)*	*(20 oz)*	*(28 oz)*	*(2 lb)*	*(2¼ lb)*	*(2½ lb)*	*(3 lb)*
Royal icing	450 g	550 g	700 g	900 g	1 kg	1.1 kg	1.4 kg	1.6 kg
	(1 lb)	*(20 oz)*	*(24 oz)*	*(2 lb)*	*(2¼ lb)*	*(2½ lb)*	*(3 lb)*	*(3½ lb)*

ROYAL ICING

Makes about 900 g (2 lb). (To calculate quantity required, see chart, left.) Keep 24 hours, covered.

4 egg whites

900 g (2 lb) icing sugar

15 ml (1 tbsp) lemon juice

10 ml (2 tsp) glycerine

1 Whisk egg whites until slightly frothy. Sift and stir in a quarter of icing sugar. Gradually add remaining three-quarters, beating well after each addition.

2 Beat in the lemon juice and continue beating for about 10 minutes until icing is smooth. Beat in remaining sugar until required consistency is achieved. Stir in glycerine to stop icing hardening.

ICING A CAKE

1 Stand the cake and board on a non-slip surface. Spoon almost half the icing on to the top of the cake and spread it evenly over the surface with a palette knife, using a paddling action.

2 Using an icing ruler or palette knife longer than the width of the cake, without applying any pressure, draw it steadily across the top of the cake at an angle of 30°. Repeat if necessary.

3 Neaten the edges by holding a palette knife upright and running it around the rim of the cake to remove surplus icing. Leave to dry for about 24 hours before applying icing to side of cake. Cover remaining icing.

4 Place cake on an icing turntable or up-turned plate. Spread remaining icing on the side and smooth roughly with a small palette knife, using a paddling action.

5 Hold the palette knife upright and at an angle of 45° to the cake. Draw the knife or comb towards you to smooth the surface. For a square cake, apply icing to each side separately. Neaten the edges with a palette knife.

6 Thin icing with a little water, and apply this as a second coat, allowing the first coat to dry for 1–2 days first. Use a sharp knife to trim off any rough icing. Brush surface with greasefree pastry brush to remove icing dust. Leave to dry.

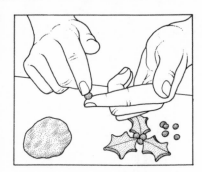

2 Make holly berries. Colour some almond paste red with a few drops of the appropriate colouring and roll into small balls.

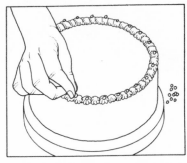

4 Place a silver ball in the centre of each of the piped stars before the icing dries.

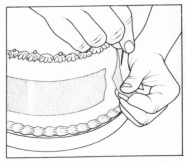

6 Place your selected piece of ribbon in position around the cake and secure the ends with headed pins.

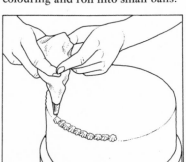

3 Using an icing bag fitted with an eight-point star nozzle and white icing, pipe a border around the top edge of the cake.

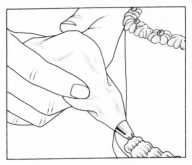

5 Using the same icing bag and nozzle as for the top edge, pipe a shell border along the base edge of the cake.

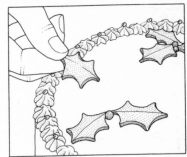

7 Arrange the holly leaves and berries on top of the cake. Pipe a little icing on the back and fix on to the cake.

DECORATIVE ICING

The icing should have been allowed to settle for 24 hours before you plan to use it (see recipe on page 149) to let the air bubbles settle, so you may need to beat it very lightly with a wooden spoon to refresh the texture. If necessary, adjust the consistency with egg white or icing sugar. Royal icing will keep for several days in a sealed container.

When it comes to designs for icing roses, you can build up quite a variety using even the most basic range of nozzles (see opposite page). Make sure you allow enough time for these decorations to dry out.

Practice makes perfect when it comes to piping the decoration on a wedding cake, so try out your skills first on a board or piece of paper, before you tackle piping on the actual surface of the cake. Take your time, follow the instructions and step-by-step illustrations carefully, and keep a steady hand.

1 Prepare icing roses. Place a little royal icing on the top of an icing nail and stick a small square of non-stick or waxed paper on top.

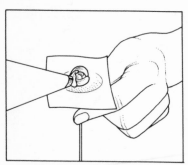

2 Place a petal nozzle in an icing bag and half-fill with white or pink royal icing. Pipe a cone of icing, twisting the nail between the thumb and forefinger, to form the centre of the icing rose.

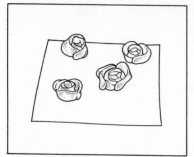

3 Pipe five or six petals around the centre of the rose, overlapping each and piping the outer petals so they are more open and lie flatter. Repeat with more roses. Dry for 24 hours on the paper.

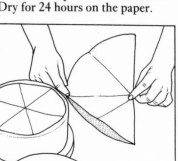

4 Cut a circle of greaseproof paper to the size of the top of each cake; fold the largest two into eight segments, the smallest into six segments.

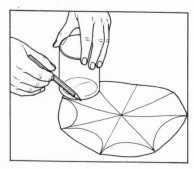

5 Using a compass or the bottom of a glass of the right diameter, pencil a scallop on the rounded edge between the folds about 5 cm (2 inches) deep for big cakes, 2.5 cm (1 inch) deep for the top tier.

6 Cut out the scallops, open paper, place on cake and hold with one hand while pricking scalloped outline on to the icing.

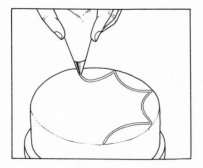

7 Remove paper and, using an icing bag filled with white icing and fitted with a plain No. 2 icing nozzle, pipe a line along the inner edge of the scallops.

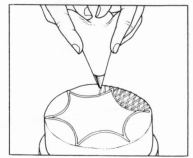

8 Then, continuing with the same nozzle as in step 7, pipe a trellis inside each scallop as shown above.

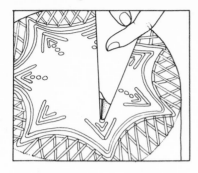

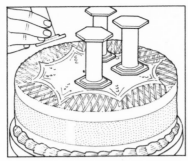

9 Using an icing bag fitted with a plain nozzle (No. 1) and white icing, pipe a line 0.5 cm ($\frac{1}{4}$ inch) outside the scalloped edge. Pipe two V's and three dots at the join of each scallop.

12 Carefully position the pillars on top of the bottom two layers of the cake and secure them with icing.

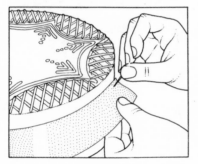

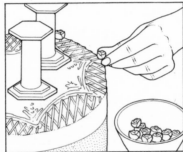

10 Place your selected pieces of ribbon in position around the cakes. Secure the ends in position with headed pins.

13 Finish the decoration with a rose at the points where the scallops meet, and clusters at the base of the pillars.

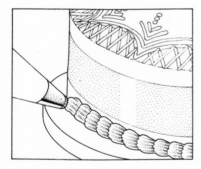

11 Using an icing bag fitted with a three-point star nozzle and white icing, pipe a shell or star border around the base of the cakes.

ICING TIPS

With even a limited number of nozzles a wide variety of designs can be built up. Select those *without* a screw collar for use with a paper icing bag. Larger nozzles of similar shape may be useful for piping icing on bigger cake designs.

- Fine plain (writing)
- Medium plain (writing)
- Thicker plain (writing)
- Six-point star
- Eight-point star (medium)
- Petal

To make a Greaseproof Icing Bag

1 Fold a 25.5-cm (10-inch) square of greaseproof paper in half diagonally, to form a triangle.

2 Take one point from the long side, fold up to meet the middle point and twist under to form a cone.

3 Holding the middle points with one hand, take the second point from the other long side and twist over the cone to meet the middle points being held together. Secure all three together with a staple to form a firm cone.

4 Cut off the very tip of the bag with a pair of scissors and drop in a plain nozzle.

5 Spoon in royal icing to little more than half full. Don't overfill the bag. Fold bag over as shown in picture to trap in icing.

Techniques of Piping

- Good results can only be achieved with practice.
- Never overfill the bag and always keep the remaining icing covered whilst piping.
- Any filled bags not in use can be kept in a plastic bag to stop crusting of the icing.

Basic Recipes

This chapter is packed with all the basic recipes you need to make up the dishes in this book. From simple things with basic methods like stocks, sauces, salads and dressings, to pastry recipes and how to prepare and cook vegetable accompaniments (there's even a whole page devoted to cooking potatoes).

MAKING PASTRY

PUFF PASTRY

Makes 900 g (2 lb)

450 g (1 lb) strong plain flour
pinch of salt
450 g (1 lb) butter
300 ml ($\frac{1}{2}$ pint) iced water
15 ml (1 tbsp) lemon juice
beaten egg, to glaze

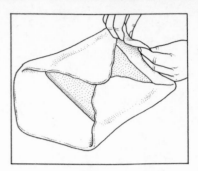

1 Mix the flour and salt together in a bowl. Cut off 50 g (2 oz) of butter and pat the remaining butter with a rolling pin into a slab 2 cm ($\frac{3}{4}$ inch) thick. Rub the 50 g (2 oz) of butter into the flour. Stir in enough water and lemon juice to make a soft dough. Knead and shape into a round.

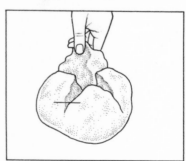

2 Cut through half the depth in the shape of a cross. Open out the flaps to form a star. Roll out, keeping the centre four times as thick as the flaps.

3 Place slab of butter in centre and fold over flaps, envelope-style. Press with a rolling pin and roll out into a rectangle measuring about 40 × 20 cm (16 × 8 inches).

4 Fold the bottom third up and the top third down, keeping the edges straight. Seal the edges by pressing with the rolling pin. Wrap the pastry in greaseproof paper and leave in the refrigerator to 'rest' for 30 minutes.

5 Put the pastry on a lightly floured working surface with the folded edges to the sides and repeat the rolling, folding and resting sequence five times. After the final resting, roll out the pastry on a lightly floured surface and shape as required. Brush with beaten egg before baking. The usual oven temperature is 230°C (450°F) mark 8 for puff pastry recipes.

FREEZING PUFF PASTRY
Pack in freezer cling film or foil in amounts that are practical to thaw and use. Thaw at room temperature for 1$\frac{1}{2}$–2 hours.

Note Uncooked home-made puff pastry will keep for 2–3 days if wrapped in foil or cling film and stored in the refrigerator.

*Bought puff pastry, either chilled or frozen, is very satisfactory, but remember to roll it out to only a maximum thickness of 3 mm ($\frac{1}{8}$ inch), as it rises well.
   One pound (flour weight) of puff pastry is equivalent to two 368-g (13-oz) packets of frozen.

SHORTCRUST PASTRY

For shortcrust pastry, use half the quantity of fat to flour. Therefore, for a recipe using quantities of shortcrust pastry other than 225 g (8 oz) simply use half the quantity of fat to flour weight specified.

| 225 g (8 oz) plain flour |
| pinch of salt |
| 50 g (2 oz) butter or block margarine |
| 50 g (2 oz) lard |

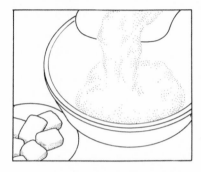

1 Sift the flour and salt together in a bowl. Cut the butter and lard into small pieces and add to the flour.

2 Lightly rub in the butter or margarine and the lard until the mixture resembles fine bread-crumbs.

3 Add 30–45 ml (2–3 tbsp) chilled water evenly over the surface and stir in until the mixture begins to stick together in large lumps.

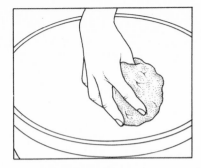

4 With one hand, collect the mixture together to form a ball. Knead lightly for a few seconds to give a firm, smooth dough. Do not over-handle.

BAKING BLIND

Baking blind is the term used to describe the cooking of pastry cases without any filling. The pastry may be partially pre-baked to be cooked again when filled, or completely cooked if filling requires no further cooking. All shortcrust pastries and puff pastries may be baked blind.

The pastry shell is pricked with a fork and then lined with foil or greaseproof paper. For larger cases, it is then filled with baking beans (that is, dried pulses, rice, or purpose-made ceramic 'beans') before cooking. Keep the beans specifically for this purpose as, although they cannot afterwards be eaten, they may, like the foil, be used again and again.

• Pastry cases which need complete pre-baking should be returned to the oven for a further 15 minutes or until the base is firm to the touch and light gold in colour.
  Cases which have been baked blind keep for several days in an airtight tin and will freeze well wrapped in freezer foil and stored in a rigid container.
• For small pastry cases, prick the pastry well with a fork and line with foil only before baking.

5 The pastry can be used straight away, but it is better if allowed to 'rest' for about 30 minutes wrapped in foil in the refrigerator.

6 Roll out the pastry on a lightly floured surface to a thickness about 3 mm ($\frac{1}{8}$ inch). Do not pull or stretch the pastry. To cook, the usual oven temperature is 200–220°C (400–425°F) mark 6–7.

To freeze: Baked and unbaked shortcrust pastry freeze well. Thaw unrolled dough at room temperature before unwrapping; rolled out pastry may be cooked from frozen, allowing extra time.

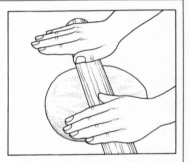

1 Roll out the pastry to a circle 5 cm (2 inches) wider than diameter of tin. Wrap pastry loosely around rolling pin and lift into tin. Unroll into position.

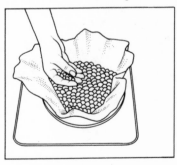

2 Press the paper against the pastry; weigh down with beans to form an even layer about 1 cm ($\frac{1}{2}$ inch) deep. For partially pre-baked cases, bake for about 10–15 minutes at 200°C (400°F) mark 6. Remove the paper and beans and bake for a further 5 minutes until set.

STOCKS

Any dish will benefit from the flavour of a good homemade stock. There is usually something in the refrigerator which will help the flavour of a stock – a carcass, giblets or scraps of meat and vegetables – and butchers are often willing to give away a few bones.

BASIC BONE STOCK

Makes about 1.1 litres (2 pints)

900 g (2 lb) meat bones, fresh or from cooked meat

cold water

2 onions

2 sticks celery, trimmed

2 carrots

5 ml (1 tsp) salt

3 peppercorns

bouquet garni or sprig of parsley and thyme, bayleaf, blade of mace, etc.

1 Wash the bones. Put in a large pot. If using a pressure cooker add 1.4 litres (2½ pints) water, bring to the boil and skim off any scum. Add roughly chopped vegetables, salt, peppercorns and spices.

2 Bring to High (15-lb) pressure and cook for 1–1¼ hours. If you are using marrow bones, increase the water to 1.7 litres (3 pints) and cook for 2 hours. Reduce pressure at room temperature. (If using an ordinary pan use 2 litres (3½ pints) water. After skimming, add the peppercorns, herbs and spices, vegetables, and simmer, well covered, for 5–6 hours.)

3 Strain the stock thoroughly, discarding the vegetables, and leave to cool. When cold, remove all traces of fat completely.

CHICKEN STOCK

Makes 1.1–1.4 litres (2–2½ pints)

1 roast chicken carcass plus scraps

1.4–1.7 litres (2½–3 pints) water

roughly chopped celery, onions and carrots

bouguet garni (optional)

Put the carcass, bones and scraps in a pan with the water, flavouring vegetables and herbs, if used. Bring to the boil, skim and simmer, covered for 3 hours. (Alternatively, pressure cook at High (15-lb) for 45–60 minutes. Strain the stock and, when cold, remove all traces of fat.

BASIC WHITE (POURING) SAUCE

Makes 300 ml (½ pint)

15 g (½ oz) butter

15 g (½ oz) plain flour

300 ml (½ pint) milk

salt and freshly ground pepper

1 Melt the butter in a saucepan. Add the flour and cook over low heat, stirring with a wooden spoon, for 2 minutes. Do not allow the mixture (roux) to brown.

2 Remove the pan from the heat and gradually blend in the milk, stirring after each addition to prevent lumps forming. Bring to the boil slowly and continue to cook, stirring all the time, until the sauce comes to the boil and thickens.

3 Once thickened, simmer the sauce very gently for a further 2–3 minutes. Season with salt and freshly ground pepper.

—————— VARIATION ——————

COATING SAUCE

Follow recipe for Pouring Sauce (see above), but increase butter and flour to 25 g (1 oz) each.

SALADS

When making a green salad, use two or more green salad ingredients, such as lettuce, mustard and cress, watercress, endive, chicory, peppers, cucumber and cabbage. Wash and drain them well and, just before serving, toss lightly in a bowl with some French dressing, adding a little finely chopped onion if liked.

RUSSIAN SALAD

Serves 8

1 small cauliflower, trimmed

100 g (4 oz) turnips, peeled

100 g (4 oz) carrots, peeled

225 g (8 oz) potatoes, peeled

1 small cooked beetroot, skinned

2 medium tomatoes, skinned

salt and freshly ground pepper

150 ml (¼ pint) mayonnaise (right)

a little lemon juice

100 g (4 oz) tongue, diced

100 g (4 oz) prawns, peeled

100 g (4 oz) peas, cooked

4 gherkins, chopped

30 ml (2 tbsp) capers

6 olives and 6 anchovies, to garnish

1 Break the cauliflower into small florets and cook in boiling salted water for about 8 minutes until tender. Drain, rinse and drain again.

2 Dice turnips, carrots and potatoes finely and cook in the same way, rinse and drain. Dice beetroot and tomatoes, discarding seeds.

3 Place a layer of cauliflower in a deep salad bowl and season well. Thin mayonnaise with lemon juice and spread a little over the cauliflower. Layer the other vegetables, tongue and prawns in the same way, ending with mayonnaise.

4 To serve, sprinkle over gherkins and capers and garnish with olives and anchovies.

COLESLAW

Serves 8

½ white cabbage, trimmed and finely shredded

1 large carrot, peeled and grated

1 large onion, skinned and finely chopped

45 ml (3 tbsp) chopped fresh parsley

4 sticks celery, trimmed and sliced

salt and freshly ground pepper

200 ml (⅓ pint) mayonnaise (see right) or salad cream

watercress, to garnish (optional)

1 In a large bowl, combine the first five ingredients, tossing well together. Season the mayonnaise or salad cream well, pour over the vegetables and toss until well coated.

2 Cover and chill in the refrigerator for 2–3 hours before serving, garnished with watercress, if wished.

POTATO SALAD

Serves 6

900 g (2 lb) potatoes

4 spring onions, trimmed and chopped

salt and freshly ground pepper

150 ml (¼ pint) mayonnaise (see right)

chopped fresh chives, to garnish

1 Place the potatoes in cold, salted water, bring to the boil and cook for 12–15 minutes until tender. Drain, remove the skins and leave until quite cold.

2 Cut the potatoes into small dice and place in a bowl. Add onions to the potatoes; season.

3 Stir mayonnaise into the potatoes and toss gently. Leave the salad to stand for at least 1 hour so that the flavours can blend. To serve, sprinkle with chopped chives.

TOMATO SALAD

Serves 6

700 g (1½ lb) ripe tomatoes, skinned

135 ml (9 tbsp) olive oil

45 ml (3 tbsp) wine vinegar

1 small garlic clove, crushed

30 ml (2 tbsp) chopped parsley

salt and freshly ground pepper

1 Slice the tomatoes thinly and arrange on six individual serving plates. Place the oil, vinegar, garlic, parsley and seasoning in a bowl or screw-topped jar and whisk or shake well together. Spoon over the tomatoes.

2 Cover the plates tightly with cling film and chill in the refrigerator for about 2 hours.

FRENCH DRESSING

Makes about 300 ml (½ pint)

75 ml (5 tbsp) red or white wine vinegar*

10 ml (2 tsp) Dijon or made English mustard

10 ml (2 tsp) salt

5 ml (1 tsp) freshly ground pepper

10 ml (2 tsp) sugar (optional)

2 garlic cloves, crushed (optional)

200 ml (⅓ pint) oil†

For a creamy dressing blend the ingredients in an electric blender or food processor. For a thinner dressing, shake in a screw-topped jar.

─── VARIATIONS ───

* Try also **tarragon vinegar** in dressings for tomatoes or potatoes; **thyme vinegar** with eggs or mushrooms; **cider vinegar** with fruits. **Lemon juice** can be substituted for vinegar as well.

† **Sunflower oil** alone or half and half with **olive oil** is pleasant. **Walnut oil** adds interest to strongly flavoured ingredients.

MAYONNAISE

Makes about 400 ml (12 fl oz)

3 egg yolks

7.5 ml (1½ tsp) dry mustard

7.5 ml (1½ tsp) salt

2.5 ml (½ tsp) freshly ground pepper

7.5 ml (1½ tsp) sugar (optional)

450 ml (¾ pint) sunflower oil or ½ olive oil and ½ vegetable oil

45 ml (3 tbsp) white wine vinegar or lemon juice

1 Put the egg yolks in a bowl with the seasonings and sugar and beat with a whisk. Continue beating and add 150 ml (¼ pint) of the oil about a drop at a time.

2 Once the mixture starts to thicken, continue in a thin stream. Add the vinegar or lemon juice, beating constantly.

3 Add the remaining oil 15 ml (1 tbsp) at a time or in a thin stream, beating continually until it is completely absorbed.

─── VARIATIONS ───

Tomato mayonnaise: Prepare as above, but add 2 tomatoes, skinned, seeded and diced; 3 small spring onions, trimmed and chopped; 3.75 ml (¾ tsp) salt and 15 ml (1 tbsp) vinegar or lemon juice.

Garlic mayonnaise: Skin 2 medium-sized garlic cloves and crush with some of the measured salt, add to the finished mayonnaise.

Cucumber mayonnaise: Prepare as above but add 90 ml (6 tbsp) finely chopped cucumber and 7.5 ml (1½ tsp) salt.

PREPARING AND COOKING VEGETABLES

The choice of vegetables available in shops today is enormous. By importing from different parts of the world at different times of year there is always a wide selection from which to choose. Buy vegetables carefully as quality is important. Bruised, damaged or old, tough vegetables can be picked over and cooked gently into soups, but for boiling and salads you need the best you can buy.

STORING AND PREPARING
Store vegetables in a cool, airy place such as a vegetable rack in a larder or in the salad drawer of a refrigerator.

Green vegetables should be used as soon as possible after buying, when their vitamin C value is at its highest. Prepare all vegetables as near to their cooking or serving time as possible to retain both flavour and nutrients. Because vitamin C is water-soluble, vegetables should not be put into water until ready to be cooked.

Serve vegetables as soon as they are cooked – they deteriorate through being kept hot. When serving more than one vegetable at a meal try to balance the colours and textures. Slightly under- rather than over-cook, to preserve nutrients and keep a good texture and colour. Steaming and stir-frying are good methods of preserving texture and flavour.

IDEAS FOR SEASONING
Add seasoning to cooked vegetables, especially if they have been steamed or fried without salt. Fresh herbs combine well if sprinkled in just before serving. Try caraway on carrots, tarragon on peas, oregano on courgettes. A little grated nutmeg improves cabbage, spinach and mashed potatoes.

GETTING THE BEST FROM GREENS

Cooked properly, stretched with all manner of ingredients – meat, fish, cheese, rice, vegetables – greens can take pride of place in a varied diet. Prepared greens will keep for a day in a damp polythene bag in the refrigerator. Home-grown greens usually need shorter cooking time than bought ones.

All greens taste better cooked with sea salt. Use about 5 ml (1 tsp) to each 300 ml ($\frac{1}{2}$ pint) water and 450 g (1 lb) greens. Don't keep greens hot after cooking; if necessary let them cool and reheat when needed. Reheat with a knob of butter and some freshly ground black pepper or grated nutmeg.

Broccoli Never buy broccoli that is yellowing. The stem snaps easily if the vegetable is fresh. To prepare, trim the stems, cut large heads and stems through lengthways and wash. The stem of calabrese (or purple 'hearting' broccoli) can be cut off to 2.5 cm (1 inch) so that the heads don't overcook. Steam or boil bundles of trimmed broccoli in a little boiling salted water for 10–15 minutes so that the stalks boil and the heads steam. When cooked the broccoli should be crisp to the bite. Drain and serve with melted butter and a squeeze of lemon juice or garnish of toasted flaked almonds. It can also be served with a rich hollandaise sauce.

Brussels sprouts need to be perfectly fresh when bought and don't keep for long. Look for firm, compact sprouts and avoid any that have a trace of yellow or that are open. Good sprouts don't need much trimming. Cut a cross on the stems of larger ones and wash them all in cold water. Use a wide, shallow pan that takes them in one layer, otherwise those underneath will over-cook. Cook for 5–8 minutes in about 2.5 cm (1 inch) of gently boiling salted water and leave the pan lid slightly open to keep a good green colour. They should still have a little crunch at the core when done. Drain thor-

oughly and toss in melted butter with nutmeg and ground pepper. They are also delicious almost cooked then fried in bacon fat with a few crumbled chestnuts. For a richer dish, turn fully cooked sprouts in gently warmed cream, then garnish with tiny fried croûtons, flaked almonds or buttered crumbs. To accompany roast chicken, purée sprouts with a spoon or two of cream, a knob of butter and generous seasoning. Cook Brussels sprouts tops as you would spring greens.

Cabbage Discard rough leaves, quarter and cut away hard core. Shred finely and wash in cold water. Use just enough salted water to cover. Add cabbage to boiling water and cook for about 5 minutes. Drain thoroughly, turn well in butter and season with pepper and nutmeg. Soured cream or natural yogurt make a good finish for cabbage.

Spinach should be young with small leaves. Allow 225 g (8 oz) per person. Tear away coarse ribs and wash well with plenty of water. Cook over moderate heat in just the water that clings to the leaves after washing and a sprinkling of salt, stirring occasionally for about 5 minutes until tender and reduced. Alternatively, boil small amounts gently in plenty of salted water for about 5 minutes, drain then press with a potato masher. Serve whole or chopped, with melted butter and grated nutmeg. Can be puréed and reheated with cream, pepper, nutmeg and a dusting of grated Parmesan cheese.

Spring greens, kale and curly kale should be bought very fresh. Discard coarse dark leaves, remove any thick ribs, shred roughly, wash. Cook spring greens in a little boiling salted water for 5 minutes; drain well. Serve with butter and nutmeg. Kale and curly kale need 10–15 minutes cooking time. To serve, drain well, press out surplus water, chop finely.

POTATOES

All potatoes taste better and keep their shape well if cooked in their skins, which also helps preserve the vitamin C content. The skins can easily be removed after cooking. If you do peel potatoes ahead of time, don't store them in water for long as some vitamins and starch will be lost.

Allow 175–225 g (6–8 oz) per portion.

DUCHESSE POTATOES

Serves 6

900 g (2 lb) potatoes
salt and freshly ground pepper
50 g (2 oz) butter or margarine
pinch of grated nutmeg
2 eggs, beaten

1 Boil the potatoes. Drain well, then sieve or mash. Beat in the butter with plenty of seasoning and a pinch of nutmeg. Gradually beat in most of the eggs, reserving a little for glazing.

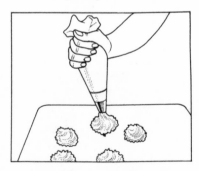

2 Cool the potato mixture then spoon into a piping bag fitted with a large star nozzle. Pipe the mixture in pyramids on to a greased baking sheet.

3 Brush carefully with the remaining egg to which a pinch of salt has been added. Bake in the oven at 200°C (400°F) mark 6 for about 25 minutes or until golden brown and set. When cooked, place in a serving dish.

SAUTÉ POTATOES

Serves 4

700–900 g (1½–2 lb) potatoes, washed
salt and freshly ground pepper
50 g (2 oz) butter or 60 ml (4 tbsp) vegetable oil

1 Cook the potatoes in boiling salted water for 15 minutes or until just tender. Drain well and remove the skins. Cut the potatoes into 0.5-cm (¼-inch) slices with a sharp knife.

2 Heat the butter or oil in a large frying pan and add the potato slices. Cook until golden brown and crisp all over. Drain well on absorbent kitchen paper and sprinkle with salt and pepper before serving.

GRATIN DAUPHINOIS

Serves 6

1.4 kg (3 lb) old potatoes, peeled
garlic clove, skinned and crushed
300 ml (10 fl oz) single cream
salt and freshly ground pepper
pinch of grated nutmeg
100 g (4 oz) Gruyère cheese, grated
watercress, to garnish

1 Cut the potatoes into small pieces and parboil for 5 minutes; drain well and place in a lightly greased pie dish or shallow casserole.

2 Stir the garlic into the cream, with the salt, pepper and nutmeg. Pour this seasoned cream over the potatoes and sprinkle with the cheese.

3 Cover with foil and bake in the oven at 180°C (350°F) mark 4 for about 1½ hours. Remove the foil and flash the gratin under the grill to brown the cheese. Serve garnished with watercress.

HASSELBACK POTATOES

Serves 8

16 potatoes, about 75 g (3 oz) each
vegetable oil
salt and freshly ground pepper

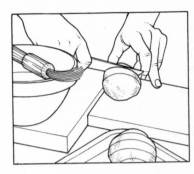

1 Peel and cut the potatoes across their width at 0.5 cm (¼ inch) intervals three-quarters of the way through.

2 Place in a single layer in an oiled baking tin. Brush with oil and season well.

3 Roast, uncovered, in the oven at 180°C (350°F) mark 4 for about 1 hour or until cooked through. Serve immediately.

ROAST POTATOES

Serves 4

700–900 g (1½–2 lb) potatoes, peeled
lard or dripping
chopped fresh parsley, to garnish

1 Cut the potatoes into evenly sized pieces, place them in cold salted water and bring to the boil. Cook for 2–3 minutes and drain.

2 Heat lard in a roasting tin in the oven. Add the potatoes, baste with the fat and cook at 220°C (425°F) mark 7 for 45 minutes or until golden brown. Sprinkle with chopped parsley.

BONING POULTRY

Absolutely essential is a small cook's knife with a very sharp blade 7.5–10 cm (3–4 inches) long. Work on a chopping board, as the knife will mark laminated surfaces. Strong scissors are needed for snipping the sinews and trimming.

To sew the bird you'll need a short darning needle or a trussing needle with a large enough eye to take fine string or separated strands of coarse string.

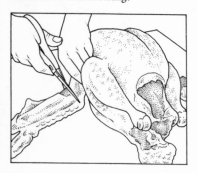

1 If using a frozen bird, first remove the giblets for the stock pot. Snip off the wing pinions at the second joint and remove the parson's nose; these go in the stock pot too. Wipe the bird well, plucking feathers or quills; pat dry.

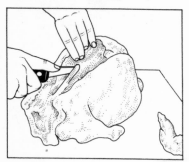

2 Resting the bird on its breast, cut straight down the back through the skin to the bone. Gradually fillet and ease flesh and skin away from the bone. Work down towards the joints, turning the bird as you go. Keep knife close to backbone and rib-cage.

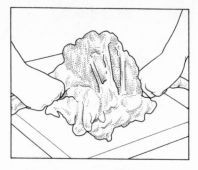

3 Clasping one leg in each hand, press very firmly outwards to release the ball and socket joints – a great deal of pressure is required. Ease the point of the knife into the joints and separate the legs from the body. Repeat for the wings.

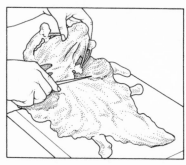

4 Return to the main body of the bird and continue filleting the flesh from the breast bone. Take care, as there is little flesh below the skin. Work down both sides of the bone and continue gently along the tip until the whole carcass can be cleanly removed. Use for the stock pot.

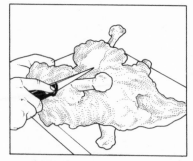

5 Taking hold of the thigh end of the leg joint in one hand, scrape the flesh down from the bone towards the hinge joint.

6 Use the point of the knife – a cartilage has to be removed too. Continue filleting the flesh off the lower leg joint until the knobbly end is reached.

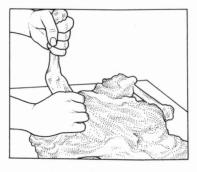

7 Clasp the exposed bones in one hand and the skin and flesh in the other. Pull the leg completely inside out to remove the bone, snipping any sinews.

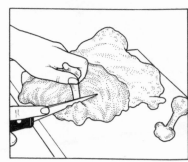

8 Remove the wings similarly, easing out any pieces of breast bone attached, and remove the wishbone.

INDEX